Mapping Clinical Value Streams

Lean Tools for Healthcare Series

Series Editor: Thomas L. Jackson

PUBLISHED

5S for Healthcare

Standard Work for Lean Healthcare

Kaizen Workshops for Lean Healthcare

Mapping Clinical Value Streams

FORTHCOMING

Just-in-Time for Healthcare

Mistake Proofing for Lean Healthcare

Mapping Clinical Value Streams

Rona Consulting Group & Productivity Press
Thomas L. Jackson

CRC Press
Taylor & Francis Group
Boca Raton   London   New York

CRC Press is an imprint of the
Taylor & Francis Group, an **informa** business

A PRODUCTIVITY PRESS BOOK

CRC Press
Taylor & Francis Group
6000 Broken Sound Parkway NW, Suite 300
Boca Raton, FL 33487-2742

© 2013 by Taylor & Francis Group, LLC
CRC Press is an imprint of Taylor & Francis Group, an Informa business

No claim to original U.S. Government works

Printed in the United States of America on acid-free paper
Version Date: 20121107

International Standard Book Number: 978-1-4665-5184-8 (Paperback)

Library of Congress Cataloging-in-Publication Data

Jackson, Thomas Lindsay, 1949-
    Mapping clinical value streams / Thomas L. Jackson.
       p. ; cm. -- (Lean tools for healthcare series)
    Includes index.
    ISBN 978-1-4665-5184-8 (pbk. : alk. paper)
    I. Title. II. Series: Lean tools for healthcare series.
    [DNLM: 1. Hospital Administration--methods. 2. Efficiency, Organizational. 3. Quality Assurance, Health Care--methods. WX 150.1]

362.11068--dc23   2012044628

**Visit the Taylor & Francis Web site at
http://www.taylorandfrancis.com**

**and the CRC Press Web site at
http://www.crcpress.com**

Contents

Preface

Since the publication of *To Err Is Human: Building a Safe Health System* by the US Institute of Medicine in 1999, the healthcare industry has been struggling to reform its clinical processes to make patients safe. Unfortunately, despite a flurry of publications and conferences, and with the exception of a few notable institutions—such as the Virginia Mason Medical Center, Park Nicollet Health Services, and Thedacare—little has been accomplished. Tens of thousands of patients die unnecessarily every year as a result of inadvertent errors and defects in our healthcare processes. Those that survive pay too much, perhaps far too much, for the privilege.

The value stream mapping method described in this book provides a powerful tool for observing and depicting processes as they truly are—and for imagining the same processes without medical errors and other costly waste. Moreover, value stream mapping accomplishes this feat from the *patient's* perspective. It permits clinicians to re-envision their work as if they had "a patient on their shoulder." As we will see in Chapter 4, we achieve this patient-centered perspective by following real, live patients as they experience the entire course of their diagnosis and treatment. (Actually, we often follow the process until the patient receives the final, correct bill, but that is a topic for another book on administrative value steam mapping. Until then, see Keyte and Locher's, *The Complete Lean Enterprise* [New York: Productivity Press, 2004].)

Value stream maps are also an excellent tool for establishing the vision and strategy to develop your business. They help you understand how your healthcare business actually works and how it might work better. The observation that the healthcare industry's costs are too high and quality too low is a very old maxim. But why is it true? And why does it remain true more than 10 years after the publication of *To Err Is Human?* Perhaps it is because we do not yet have a complete diagnosis. Judging from the healthcare industry's high costs and poor quality record, the patient's perspective is not necessarily contemplated in our schools of medicine, nursing, or healthcare management. *Mapping Clinical Value Streams* has been written specifically to help your organization apply the concepts of value, flow, and pull, which have been highly effective in the improvement of manufacturing processes, to healthcare processes.

As a Lean evangelist in the world of healthcare, I am reminded daily that healthcare is different from manufacturing. This is true. It has also led to a number of problems translating the manufacturing language of value stream mapping into a natural-sounding healthcare idiom. Several difficulties arise because patients play a dual role: (1) patient as customer and (2) patient as participant in the system. From the patient-as-customer perspective, it is patently obvious that clinicians must be patient centered, kind, and compassionate. From the patient-as-participant perspective, it is not so clear.

And patients become participants in healthcare processes in the sense that they are key "inputs" to those processes. Once a patient signs a consent form, she consigns herself to becoming an input more or less like any other. This does not mean that patients sign away their right to be treated as human beings. Rather, it means that patients recognize that healthcare services are performed upon the human body, without which no medicine or procedure can take effect. Healthcare professionals are not comfortable viewing the patient in this way; but patients will likely tell you that the healthcare industry does not hesitate to treat them this way. Patients neglected in a waiting room are like so many parts on a shelf.

Ironically, perhaps, in the act of viewing the patient as a key participant in the processes of healthcare (that is, by viewing the patient as an input instead of a customer), we gain the patient's perspective that has been lacking for so long. In mapping the processes of healthcare, we will follow—*literally*—real patients as they wait in the doctor's office, as they receive their diagnoses, and as they travel to the lab for tests, to preop, to surgery, to recovery, and home. By viewing the patient as a key participant, we will learn firsthand why it is that 70% or more of healthcare defects occur in the hand-offs from doctor to nurse, from hospital to lab, and from nurse to patient. And we will observe many opportunities to make the healthcare system function much more effectively for patients and clinicians alike.

Another set of difficulties arises because patients frequently do not know what to ask for when they first enter a healthcare process. In other words, customer requirements are unclear. This is what the diagnostic process is intended to reveal. In a sense, although the patient may have consented to be a key participant (patient as input) the patient as customer still retains the right to "change her mind," as it were. Consequently, as clinicians learn more about the condition of a patient, there can be unexpected changes in the schedules for the production of healthcare services. Fortunately, the value stream mapping language of "pull production" is robust enough to accommodate the need to reschedule production for all types of reasons.

The information in *Mapping Clinical Value Streams* is presented in a highly organized and easy-to-assimilate format. There are numerous illustrations to reinforce the text. Margin assists call your attention to key points and other important features. Value stream mapping icons make it easy to see and understand the ebb and flow of healthcare processes. And throughout the book you are asked to reflect on questions that will help you apply these concepts and techniques to your own workplace. Each chapter has a summary for quick review.

To be competitive in today's marketplace, you absolutely cannot afford to leave processes unexamined or let them be haphazard or become customary by default. You must apply conscious, quality attention to see and fix your healthcare processes. *Mapping Clinical Value Streams* shows you how.

Acknowledgments

First, I want to thank John Shook and Mike Rother, authors of *Learning to See* (Brookline, MA Lean Enterprise Academy, 1998), the book that started the value stream mapping craze in manufacturing more than a decade ago. They set a very high bar. Second, I must thank Marc Baker and Ian Taylor for their groundbreaking book, *Making Hospitals Work* (Herefordshire, UK: Lean Enterprise Academy, 2009). I must also thank Dan Jones, whose keynote presentation at the 2011 Lean Society Summit in Italy made me aware of the Lean Enterprise Academy's groundbreaking work in healthcare and made me realize that *Mapping Clinical Value Streams* should be included in the Lean Tools for Healthcare series. I also thank my client and friend Mario Nardi, president of the CUOA Lean Enterprise Club, for inviting me to participate in the summit. Next, I thank my partner, Mike Rona, for insisting that I write the book. Finally, the development of *Mapping Clinical Value Streams* has been a team effort. Daksha Jackson of 6 Penang Street helped with the initial development of the draft. Maura May, the Lean Tools for Healthcare series project manager, helped me with the developmental edits. Heidi Butenschoen of Gehrschoen Creative helped with the artwork. Mike Rona, Patti Crome, Erin Ressler, Dr. Sam Carlson, Susie Creger, Ann Kernan, Miwa Kudo, Jim Bevier, and Dahlia Mak of the Rona Consulting Group gave valuable feedback on the content of the book.

We are very pleased to bring you this addition to our Lean Tools for Healthcare series and wish you continued and increasing success on your Lean journey.

Thomas L. Jackson

Chapter 1

Getting Started

1.1 THE PURPOSE OF THIS BOOK

Key Point

Mapping Clinical Value Streams was written to give you the information you need to map the processes of healthcare in all of its clinical settings—from the outpatient clinic to the emergency department to the operating room, through the inpatient stay, to physical therapy and beyond. You are a valued member of your healthcare organization's transformation team; your knowledge, support, and participation are essential to the success of any major improvement effort in your organization.

You may be reading this book because your team leader or manager asked you to do so. Or you may be reading it because you think it will provide information that will help you in your work. By the time you finish Chapter 1, you will have a better idea of how the information in this book can help you and your organization eliminate waste and serve your patients more effectively.

1.2 WHAT THIS BOOK IS BASED ON

Background INFO

This book is about value stream mapping, an approach to visualizing healthcare processes in order to identify and eliminate non-value-added activities, or waste. The methods and goals discussed here are closely related to the Lean system developed at Toyota Motor Company. Since 1979, Productivity Press has published knowledge and information about these approaches. Since 2007, the Rona Consulting Group has been applying the knowledge to the work of healthcare. Today, top organizations around the world are applying Lean healthcare principles to improve patient safety and make healthcare more affordable.

1.3 TWO WAYS TO USE THIS BOOK

There are at least two ways to use this book:

- As the reading material for a learning group or study group process within your organization
- For learning on your own

Your organization may decide to design its own learning group process based on *Mapping Clinical Value Streams*. Or, you may read this book for individual learning without formal group discussion. Either way, you will find valuable concepts and techniques to apply to your daily work.

1.4 HOW TO GET THE MOST OUT OF YOUR READING

1.4.1 Become Familiar with This Book

How-to Steps There are a few steps you can follow to make it easier to absorb the information in this book. Take as much time as you need to become familiar with the material. First, get a "big picture" view of the book by doing the following:

1. Scan the table of contents to see how *Mapping Clinical Value Streams* is arranged.
2. Read the rest of this introductory section for an overview of the book's contents.
3. Flip through the book to get a feel for its style, flow, and design. Notice how the chapters are structured and glance at the illustrations.

1.4.2 Become Familiar with Each Chapter

How-to Steps After you have a sense of the overall structure of *Mapping Clinical Value Streams,* prepare yourself to study one chapter at a time. For each chapter, we suggest you follow these steps to get the most out of your reading:

1. Flip through the chapter, looking at the way it is laid out. Notice the bold headings and the key points flagged in the margins.
2. Now read the chapter. How long this takes depends on what you already know about the content and what you are trying to get out of your reading. Enhance your reading by doing the following:
   - Use the margin assists to help you follow the flow of information.
   - If the book is your own, use a highlighter to mark key information and answers to your questions about the material. If the book is not your own, take notes on a separate piece of paper.
   - Answer the "Take Five" questions in the text. These will help you absorb the information by reflecting on how you might apply it to your own workplace.
3. Read the summary at the end of the chapter to reinforce what you have learned. If you read something in the summary that you do not remember having read, find that section in the chapter and review it.
4. Finally, read the questions in the "Reflections" section at the end of the chapter. Think about these questions and write down your answers.

1.4.3 How a Reading Strategy Works

When reading a book, many people think they should start with the first word and read straight through until the end. This is not usually the best way to learn from a book. The steps that were just presented for how to read this book are a strategy for making your reading easier, more fun, and more effective.

Reading strategy is based on two simple points about the way people learn. The first point is this: *It is difficult for your brain to absorb new information if it does not have a structure within which to place it.* As an analogy, imagine trying to build a house without first putting up a framework.

Like building a frame for a house, you can give your brain a framework for the new information in the book by getting an overview of the contents and then flipping through the material. Within each chapter, you repeat this process on a smaller scale by reading the key points and headings before reading the text.

The second point about learning is this: *It is a lot easier to learn if you take in the information one layer at a time, instead of trying to absorb it all at once.* It is like finishing the walls of a house: First you lay down a coat of primer. When it is dry, you apply a coat of paint and, later, a final finish coat.

1.4.4 Using the Margin Assists

As you have noticed by now, this book uses small images called *margin assists* to help you follow the information in each chapter. There are six types of margin assists:

Background information sets the stage for what comes next.

Overview presents new information without the detail presented later.

Definition explains how the author uses key terms.

Key point highlights important ideas to remember.

New tool helps you apply what you have learned.

Example helps you understand the key points.

How-to steps give you a set of directions for using new instruments.

Principle explains how things work in a variety of situations.

1.5 AN OVERVIEW OF THE CONTENTS

1.5.1 Chapter 1: Getting Started

This chapter has already explained the purpose of *Mapping Clinical Value Streams* and how it was written. Then it shared tips for getting the most out of your reading. Now, it will present a brief description of each chapter.

1.5.2 Chapter 2: The Production Processes and Operations of Healthcare

Chapter 2 describes the industrial origins of the Lean healthcare methodology and the critical distinction between healthcare processes and operations. It also presents the five key principles of Lean healthcare management.

1.5.3 Chapter 3: Value Streams and the Mapping Process

Chapter 3 defines the key terms: value, value added, and waste. It discusses the role of the patient in the healthcare value stream, describes the seven "flows" of healthcare, and lays out the essential steps of the value stream mapping process.

1.5.4 Chapter 4: Map the Current State

Chapter 4 presents how to build a current-state map by following patients and clinicians through the process of receiving and delivering healthcare services. Chapter 4 also introduces the key terms takt time, cycle time, wait time, and lead time.

1.5.5 Chapter 5: Map the Future State: Phase I—Flow

Chapter 5 shows how to envision and create processes in which patients do not wait for healthcare services. The focus of Chapter 5 is on the construction of healthcare production units called "cells" that are capable of keeping pace with patient demand.

1.5.6 Chapter 6: Map the Future State: Phase II—Pull

In Chapter 6 we will see how to link discrete healthcare cells (processes) together into a value stream by teaching downstream processes to signal to upstream processes that they are ready to provide healthcare services. If we have organized the slowest process—sometimes called the "pacemaker"—into a cell capable of keeping pace with demand, then the entire value stream is capable of keeping pace too.

1.5.7 Chapter 7: Implement the Future State

Chapter 7 describes how to break a future-state value stream map into practical "loops" for purposes of implementation. In addition, Chapter 7 discusses the A3 process that is used to pursue perfection.

1.5.8 Chapter 8: Reflections and Conclusions

Chapter 8 presents reflections on and conclusions to this book. It also describes opportunities for further learning about techniques related to mapping and management of clinical value streams.

Chapter 2

The Production Processes and Operations of Healthcare

2.1 THE INDUSTRIAL ORIGINS OF LEAN HEALTHCARE

The purpose of the Lean Tools for Healthcare series is to introduce readers to a set of methods that have been proven to increase patient safety and dramatically reduce the cost of providing healthcare services. The term "Lean" was coined to express the notion that, like an athlete, an organization should be without organizational "fat" or what Lean specialists refer to as non-value-added waste, where value refers to what a patient would be willing to pay for. Figure 2.1 lists seven distinct types of waste found in healthcare.

Background INFO
Lean tools and methods have important origins in the United States but were perfected principally within the Toyota Motor Company between 1948 and 1963, and they have since been copied by most sectors of the manufacturing industry. The first major implementation in the healthcare industry began in 2001, when the Virginia Mason Medical Center in Seattle, Washington, engaged consultants (most of whom had been production engineers from Toyota and the Boeing Aircraft Company) to teach them how to apply the Toyota production system to the production of healthcare services. A few years later, another major implementation was launched by Park Nicollet Health Services in Minneapolis, Minnesota, and a few other organizations, including Thedacare in Wisconsin. The success of these implementations is well documented.[*]

Naturally, readers coming to the subject of "Lean healthcare" for the first time are often perplexed by the patently industrial point of view taken by Lean healthcare specialists. How can healthcare be treated as an industrial process? Is medicine not an art? Can healthcare processes be standardized when all patients are unique? In fact, medicine and healthcare practice are generally becoming

---

[*] John Black with David Miller, *The Toyota Way to Healthcare Excellence: Increase Efficiency and Improve Quality with Lean* (Chicago: Health Administration Press, 2008).

Definitions	Healthcare wastes	Administrative wastes
1. Overproduction Producing more, sooner, or faster than is required by the next process	Performing services that patients don't need or desire. Unnecessary backups between departments. Multiple quality control checks.	Printing or processing reports, emails, or other information products before they are needed. Overdissemination of reports, etc.
2. Waiting Time delays, process idle time	Waiting for lab results. Waiting for doctors. Waiting for nurses. Waiting for decisions from hospital administrators. Idle people.	Searching for information. Waiting for information system response. Waiting for approvals from superiors.
3. Transportation Unnecessary handling or transportation; multiple handling	Excessive medical record pickups and deliveries. Extra handoffs. Excess patient transfer/movement.	Transferring data files between incompatible computer systems or software packages. Overdissemination of reports, etc.
4. Overprocessing Unnecessary processing, steps, or work elements/ procedures	Asking the patient the same question 20 times. Multiple signatures. Extra copies of same form. Duplicate data input entries.	Re-entering data, extra copies; reformatting or excessive/custom formatting. Unnecessary reviews. Ccs on emails.
5. Inventory Producing, holding, or purchasing unnecessary inventory	Cabinets full of gloves. Piles of paper forms. Too many suture materials. Too many prosthetic devices. Multiple storage sites.	Decisions in process. Outdated, obsolete information in file cabinets or stored in databases.
6. Motion Excessive handling, unnecessary steps, nonergonomic motion	Long reach/walk distances. Lifting more than 35 pounds, etc. Standing all day. Sitting all day. Not enough printers. Not enough copiers.	Repetitive stress injuries resulting from poor keyboard design. Excessive walking to and from remote printers.
7. Defects Rework, correction of errors, quality problems, equipment problems	Adverse events. High infection rates. Wrong meds. Wrong surgical site. Frequent rescheduling. Patient readmissions.	Order-entry errors. Too many bill rejects. Design errors and engineering change orders. Invoice errors. Info system downtime.

Figure 2.1 The seven wastes. (From J. Michael Rona and Associates, LLC, doing business as Rona Consulting Group, copyright 2008–2013. http://www.ronaconsulting .com. All rights reserved. Reprinted with permission.)

more scientific or evidence based, and the Centers for Medicare & Medicaid Services (CMS) and deeming authorities such as the Joint Commission are quick to require adherence to standardized, evidence-based practices. Moreover, industrial engineering has long been applied to healthcare processes. Some readers may recall actor Clifton Web's portrayal of the time-and-motion consultant Frank Gilbreth in the movie *Cheaper by the Dozen*. A portion of the movie depicts Gilbreth's groundbreaking time-and-motion studies of surgery in hospital operating rooms. In many ways, the practice of Lean healthcare continues in the tradition of Gilbreth's time studies. The major difference is that the studies are not carried out by consultants; the studies are conducted by members of the healthcare team (clinicians and support staff), frequently with the voluntary participation of patients themselves.

2.2 PRODUCTION, PROCESS, AND OPERATION

Before studying Lean healthcare, you must understand precisely how the notion of "production" applies to the production of healthcare services.* As perplexing as it may seem, production is not necessarily an activity that requires machines.

Production is the making of either a product or a service—it does not matter which. Obviously, artisans produced goods and services before the advent of steam power. In its most general sense, production is simply a network of what industrial engineers call processes and operations.

A process is a sequence of cycles of work called "operations." An operation is a work cycle defined by a sequence of component tasks.

Figure 2.2 illustrates how a healthcare process—transforming a patient from the state of "unhealthy" to "healthy"—is accomplished through a series of medical and other healthcare operations. When we look at a healthcare process over time (especially when we see it from the patient's perspective), we see flows of patients, clinicians, medicines, supplies, equipment, and information in time

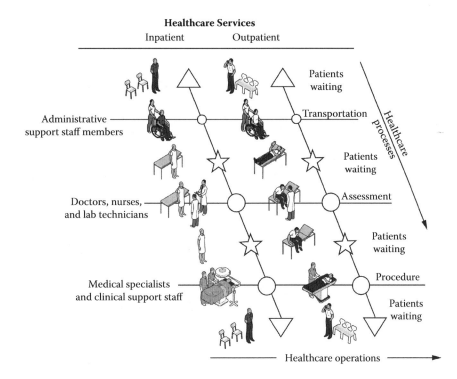

Figure 2.2 The healthcare service production process. (From J. Michael Rona and Associates, LLC, doing business as Rona Consulting Group and iStockphoto LP, copyright 2008–2013. http://www.ronaconsulting.com and http://istockphoto.com. All rights reserved. Reprinted with permission.)

---

* Much of this chapter paraphrases, in language friendly to healthcare, Chapter 1 of Shigeo Shingo's groundbreaking book, *A Study of the Toyota Production System from an Industrial Engineering Perspective* (Cambridge, MA: Productivity Press, 1989).

and space. We see the transformation of the patient from the moment at which he or she presents undiagnosed symptoms to initial assessment, definitive diagnosis, and finally treatment and recovery. When we look at operations, on the other hand, we see the work performed by doctors, nurses, lab technicians, pharmacists, etc., to accomplish this transformation—the interaction of patients, clinicians, medications, information, supplies, and equipment in time and space.

Key Point

To make fundamental improvement in the process of producing healthcare services, we must distinguish the flow of patients (process) from the clinical work flow (operation) and analyze them separately. This is why in Figure 2.2 we have illustrated healthcare production as a network of processes and operations. The analysis of healthcare *processes* examines the flow of patients; the analysis of healthcare *operations* examines the work performed on patients by clinicians and support staff.

Example

Consider a typical patient, a patient who makes a visit to an outpatient clinic: First, the patient is registered at the front desk and then asked to wait. Next, a medical assistant calls the patient and escorts him or her to an examination room. The medical assistant may take the patient's blood pressure and ask questions to make an initial assessment of the patient's condition. Again the patient is asked to wait until the doctor is ready. Finally, the doctor interviews the patient and reaches a diagnosis. After this, the patient receives some treatment—say, an injection administered by a nurse who first draws the prescribed medication and, after cleaning the patient's injection site, injects the medication into the patient's bloodstream. This series of changes in the patient (from undiagnosed to treated) is the process. The nurse's actions of filling the syringe, cleaning the patient's injection site, and injecting the medication into the patient constitute a single operation within the process. In the healthcare industry, such operations are often referred to as "protocols."

2.3 PRINCIPLES OF LEAN HEALTHCARE MANAGEMENT

Definition

Lean management is the decentralized organization of management control structures to promote the discovery, correction, anticipation, and prevention of process defects and the errors and abnormalities that result in defects.

In the broadest sense, Lean healthcare can be explained in terms of five principles that define what we may call the DNA of Lean healthcare management:

1. Standard work
2. Autonomation
3. Flow production
4. PDCA (plan–do–check–act)
5. Socratic method

These five principles are summarized in Figure 2.3.

1. Standard work	All work should be organized as standardized sequences of standardized tasks performed within a standard time and supported by a standardized amount of work in process.
2. Autonomation	When defects occur, the process should stop until the defect is corrected. Where necessary, employ mistake-proofing checklists or devices to promote critical thinking about problems in the work.
3. Flow	Ideally, patients should flow through operations and processes without interruption and without waiting.
4. PDCA	When problems occur, they should be resolved *at the source* using the scientific method of PDCA (plan–do–check–act). "At the source" means close to where the problem originally occurred, which is normally far away from where it was eventually detected.
5. Socratic method	Leaders should employ the Socratic method of questioning to develop their people as scientific problem solvers.

Figure 2.3 Five principles of Lean management.

2.3.1 Standard Work

Principle

The first principle of Lean management is that all activity—whether clinical or administrative—is governed by means of standard work. *Standard work is defined as standardized tasks performed in a standardized sequence in a standardized amount of time and with a standardized amount of medicines, supplies, and equipment to support it.* Standard work has two functions. First, it reduces variation by bringing processes into statistical process control (i.e., the quality rate $\geq$ 3-sigma). When a process is in statistical control, the process has become predictable and we can stop fighting fires. Right now, most healthcare processes are significantly out of control at 2-sigma or probably lower. Second, standard work establishes controlled conditions for small tests of change using PDCA (see later discussion). Because controlled processes are predictable, we can concentrate on preventing defects in the future. For more information about standard work and how to implement it, see *Standard Work for Lean Healthcare* (T. L. Jackson, editor, New York: Productivity Press, 2012).

2.3.2 Autonomation

Definition

The second principle of Lean management governs how different operations in a process are linked together. This principle is known as *autonomation* or, in Japanese, *jidoka. Autonomation is defined as stopping the process to build in quality.* Autonomation means essentially two things. First, we never send defects downstream to the next operation in the process; we must stop to fix defects immediately. Second, to increase the speed at which we discover and fix defects, we build inspection into each critical step of the process with checklists (such as the World Health Organization's Surgical Safety Checklist) and other "mistake-proofing" devices. For more information about jidoka and mistake proofing, see *Mistake Proofing for Lean Healthcare.* (T. L. Jackson, editor, New York: Productivity Press, forthcoming 2013). In all hand-offs from upstream to downstream operations and processes, there must be *zero ambiguity* about what the downstream operations and processes need from the upstream operations and processes that supply them.

2.3.3 Flow Production

Definition

The third Lean principle is flow production. *Flow means treating patients one at a time, with clinicians and support staff passing the patient from one step in the process to the next without inconveniencing him or her to wait or travel long distances.* Flow is always the most efficient way to deliver healthcare services. A good example of flow in healthcare is the production of healthcare services for trauma victims. Flow can only happen when the downstream process serving the patient is ready. If the patient moves before that operation or process is ready, the patient will have to wait for the downstream operation. Flow is the natural outcome of eliminating the seven non-value-added wastes in Figure 2.1. It is the ideal state of an orderly production process. Think of flow as the antichaos principle.

Flow production has a corollary principle known as pull. In cases where it is not possible for patients to flow through a healthcare process because of an acute medical condition or for any other reason, we will ask them to wait a short time, under the appropriate level of care, until the downstream process is ready to "pull" them.

2.3.4 PDCA

Chris Argyris, father of the learning organization concept, once described organizational learning as a process of detecting and correcting defects. One might say that a learning organization is an organization that finds defects and fixes them. A *Lean* organization is an organization that *anticipates* defects and *prevents* them through a process of what Argyris described as "double-loop" learning. Single-loop learning is the repeated attempt to solve a problem, with no variation of method and without questioning the goal. Double-loop learning is the ability to modify organizational methods or even goals in the light of experience. The method by which double-loop learning is accomplished within the Lean enterprise is the scientific method, summarized by the Deming cycle, or PDCA (plan–do–check–act). We will explore PDCA in more depth in Chapter 7.[*]

---

[*] For Argyris's comments about detecting and correcting defects, see M. Crossan, "Altering Theories of Learning and Action: An Interview with Chris Argyris," *Academy of Management Executive* 17 (2): 40 (2003). On double-loop learning, see Chris Argyris and Dan Schön, *Organizational Learning: A Theory of Action Perspective* (Reading, MA: Addison–Wesley, 1978).

2.3.5 Socratic Method

The fifth and final Lean principle is the Socratic method. Lean processes are highly—some say *radically*—decentralized. In order to fix defects and maintain flow, clinicians and support staff must be both qualified and empowered to make decisions in real time. Otherwise, the time between discovery and correction of defects will grow indefinitely as permission to change the process is chased up the chain of command. Obviously, this cannot be done without support from leaders, but that goes beyond management support in the traditional sense. In a Lean organization, leaders must be teachers that have mastered what is perhaps the most demanding and effective teaching method ever conceived: the Socratic method. Teachers (sometimes called *sensei*) use the Socratic method to encourage students to develop their own problem-solving powers by posing a series of open-ended questions rather than giving answers.

2.4 SUMMARY

All healthcare production carried out in any healthcare setting—in the operating room, the clinic, the lab, or the pharmacy—must be understood as a functional network of process and operation. Healthcare processes transform unwell patients into well patients. Healthcare operations are the clinical actions that accomplish those transformations. These fundamental concepts and their relationship must be understood in order to make effective, evidence-based improvements in the production of healthcare services.

Lean management, which involves decentralized management control structures designed to prevent errors and defects, is based on five key principles: standard work, autonomation, flow production, PDCA, and the Socratic method.

2.5 REFLECTIONS

Now that you have completed this chapter, take 5 minutes to think about these questions and write down your answers:

- What did you learn from reading this chapter that stands out as being particularly useful or interesting to you in healthcare?
- How do you feel about the idea of "producing" healthcare services using industrial methods?
- Do you have any questions about the topics presented in this chapter? If so, what are they?
- Are there any special obstacles in your mind or the minds of your colleagues to applying the distinction between process and operation or the five key principles of Lean management in healthcare?

- What information do you still need to understand fully the ideas presented?
- How can you get this information?
- Whom do you need to involve in this process?

Chapter 3

Value Streams and the Mapping Process

3.1 MAPPING CLINICAL VALUE STREAMS

Definition

A clinical value stream is broadly defined as the sequence of clinical processes required to provide integrated medical care to a patient diagnosed with a specific illness, including the diagnostic processes necessary to determine the requirements of the patient's care plan and the clinical service-production processes by which the care plan is executed. Ancillary processes such as diagnostic and imaging and nonclinical processes such as food and financial services are obviously critical in the diagnosis and treatment of a patient.

It will be more productive, however, to begin with the patient's progress through the main processes of healthcare—the clinical processes such as outpatient and inpatient care. Clinical processes are in effect supported by ancillary and nonclinical processes. In manufacturing, we refer to supporting processes as "feeder lines" because they "feed into" the main flow of the production process, and in manufacturing the mapping of feeder lines is normally postponed until the main flow of production has been understood. Likewise, in this book we will focus on the main flow of production—namely, the flow through the clinical processes of healthcare; we will not examine ancillary or nonclinical processes. See Figure 3.1.

Example

In Figure 3.2 we see a simplified clinical value stream for a patient who has been injured in an automobile accident. The patient's experience begins with a trip to the emergency department, after which he is admitted to the hospital for a short inpatient stay and then discharged home.

Healthcare organizations often organize their clinical processes into organizational divisions known as "service lines." This is very often a good place to start with value stream mapping. In Chapter 4 we will begin the mapping process by following a patient through multiple healthcare operations in a single clinical process or service line. In Chapter 5, we will show how to define service line operations and processes that flow, by eliminating non-value-added waste and implementing standard work. Having achieved flow within a

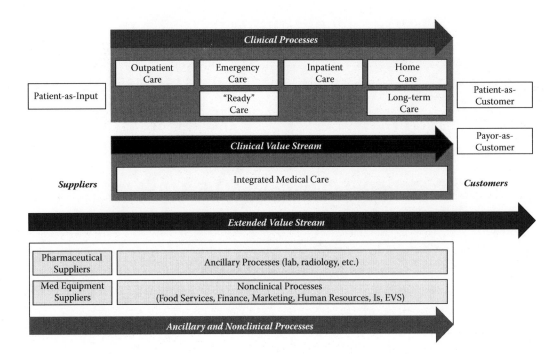

Figure 3.1 Clinical processes are supported by ancillary and nonclinical processes.

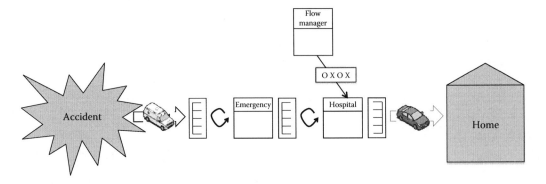

Figure 3.2 A simplified value stream map.

single service line, you will be able to zoom out and take a more panoramic view. In Chapter 6, we will show how to knit clinical processes and service lines together into integrated healthcare value streams by implementing pull systems. See Figure 3.3.

3.2 WHAT IS VALUE?

While the patient may be a key participant in a healthcare process, he or she is also still very much a customer. The philosophy of Lean healthcare management and the method of value stream mapping depend upon the concept of *value*, which has been borrowed from the academic discipline of economics.

In economics, value is defined as the price a person is willing to pay in exchange for goods or services. Lean healthcare management in general and

Definition

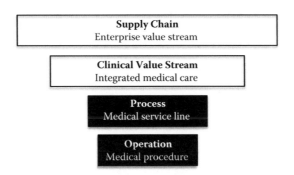

Figure 3.3 The hierarchy of operations, processes, and value streams.

value stream mapping in particular use the concept of value to analyze healthcare production in great detail, at the levels of process, individual operation, and discrete task that make up the patient's diagnosis and treatment. A *valuable activity* is something for which a patient would be willing to pay. In healthcare, of course, the government and insurance companies often pay the bill. We could have a robust discussion about how the public or private insurer's perspective on value might differ from the patient's. For the sake of simplicity, we will assume that, generally speaking, both public and private insurers have the patient's interest at heart and that their views on value are aligned. So, *value is the price that the patient is willing to pay for diagnosis and treatment.* Moreover, the concept of value can be applied to the individual activities that make up diagnostic and treatment services.

Definition

Key Point

Based upon these criteria, it stands to reason that a caregiving activity is value added if it changes the course of the patient's disease process in a way that is helpful to the patient's recovery or if it improves the patient's comfort and sense of well-being. Correctly diagnosing a patient with diabetes, injecting life-saving medication, educating the patient about her disease process, and bathing a patient are all clear examples of value-added caregiving activities because either the patient or his insurer should be willing to pay for them.*

Key Point

Conversely, an activity is non value added if it does not change the course of the patient's disease process in a helpful way or improve the patient's comfort and sense of well-being. For example, the activities of waiting for the doctor, receiving a wrong diagnosis, or receiving the wrong medication are non value added. Clearly, neither the patient nor the patient's insurer would be willing to pay for these activities. As we will see later, we can quantitatively measure non-value-added activities literally as *a waste of time.*

---

* In manufacturing, we say that an activity is value added if it changes the *form, fit, or function* of the product in a way that is helpful to the customer. In a sense, value-added healthcare activities change the form, fit, and/or function of the patient's body to combat an illness or disease process to restore or improve health.

3.3 THE SEVEN WASTES AND THE PURPOSE OF VALUE STREAM MAPPING

Definition
Waste is anything that does not add value to the process of creating or delivering a healthcare service. As discussed in Chapter 2, there are seven types of waste: overproduction, waiting, inventory, defects, transportation, overprocessing, and motion. (See Figure 2.1 in Chapter 2.)

The purpose of value stream mapping is first to identify and then to remove all non-value-added activity (waste) from a process. For many years in manufacturing and, more recently, in healthcare, the focus on waste elimination has proved to be a very effective way to decrease cost significantly while radically improving quality. In manufacturing, removing waste improves quality, cost, and on-time delivery (the so-called QCDs). In healthcare, we might say that removing waste additionally improves the three *A*s:

- Appropriateness, or safe, high-quality care delivered at the right time
- Access, which can only occur when the high costs of healthcare are brought under control
- Accountability in real time, using the A3 system (discussed in Chapter 8)

Take Five

Take 5 minutes to think about these questions and to write down your answers:

1. What do you think might be an example of a clinical value stream in your healthcare facility?
2. What do you do that is value added?
3. What are some non-value-added activities that take place in your operations? Try to name one in each of the seven categories of waste.

3.4 PATIENT AS CUSTOMER VERSUS PARTICIPANT

There are many differences between the manufacturing industry, where value stream mapping was invented, and the healthcare industry. One of these differences is the existence of "the patient," who plays a dual role in the production process. The patient is, at the same time, a customer of healthcare services and an input that is transformed by the healthcare process. As a customer, the patient receives healthcare services in exchange for payment, made directly by the patient or on behalf of the patient by a government or private insurer.

When we talk about value, value added, and non value added, we are of course thinking of the patient as customer. But the patient has another role. Because healthcare services frequently involve various tests and treatments applied to the patient's body, the patient as participant becomes a physical input to the process. Apart from being conscious, the patient as input is analogous to raw material being transformed into final product on a manufacturing production line. This dual role is not unique to healthcare. Hair and tattoo salons, for example, have customers who are also "conscious inputs" to the process. In healthcare, however, pain is often associated with treatment. Beyond this, the customer's life is sometimes at risk, so the distinction is highly charged emotionally. The patient is nevertheless a production input as well as a customer, and this must be borne in mind when building a value stream map. Essentially, the transformation process in healthcare is from illness to health, less informed to more informed, and worried and fearful to more comfortable.

3.5 WHAT IS A VALUE STREAM?

Definition

A value stream is a collection or set of processes and operations—together with their constituent skilled people, methods, materials, medication, and equipment—required to provide a well-defined family of deliverables. Value stream mapping helps us visualize an entire flow of service production and delivery from beginning to end. Traditional management methods tend to focus on isolated or functional operations within the process, such as the work of a nurse, physician, or lab technician. Because value stream maps focus on total systems, they are an excellent tool to identify and describe improvements that are needed to achieve organizational goals, as opposed to the narrowly specified goals of functional managers.

The Seven Flows of Healthcare

The method of value stream mapping is quite general and can be used to map what are known as the seven "flows" of healthcare:

1. Patients
2. Clinicians
3. Medications
4. Supplies
5. Equipment
6. Process engineering (construction of new facilities or processes)
7. Information

This book will concentrate on *clinical value streams* that follow the flows of patients through a series of clinical healthcare processes and operations as described in Figure 2.2 in Chapter 2. At the same time, we will be mapping the flows of clinicians as they attend to their patients as well as the flows of information vital to the production process moving forward in a safe and timely manner.

"Flows" in the sense of the seven flows refers generally to the repetition of any series of operations and processes. Initially, these flows are often interrupted and therefore are not "continuous flows" in the sense that we will examine later in Chapter 5. The point to value stream mapping is to map the flows in order to identify and repair discontinuities and achieve continuous flow.

Take Five

Take 5 minutes to think about these questions and to write down your answers:

1. How do you feel about considering the patient as an input in healthcare processes as well as a customer?
2. Why is value stream mapping a useful tool for improvement?

3.6 THE VALUE STREAM MAPPING PROCESS

These are the four basic steps of the process of value stream mapping (see Figure 3.4):

How-to Steps

1. Define the value that the process delivers to the patient by specifying a *service family.*
2. Build and analyze a *current-state map.*
3. Brainstorm and build a *future-state map* that establishes flow wherever possible and—where flow is not possible—links islands of flow together with a *pull system.*
4. Implement and perfect improvements.

Definition

A service family in healthcare is a set of healthcare services that tend to consume a similar constellation of resources: skilled clinicians, medication, equipment, physical spaces, etc.

Figure 3.4 Value stream mapping overview.

Definition

A current-state map describes the essential operations of healthcare processes as they currently are practiced; the map is then used to identify systematically which activities are value added and which are waste.

Definition

A future-state map describes the same process, but with the waste removed. The purpose of building a future-state map is threefold:

1. The team can envision dramatic improvements in lead time, customer satisfaction, staff satisfaction, safety, quality, inventory, productivity, capital investment, and unit cost that make a Lean enterprise so powerful. A future-state map normally assumes that you have significantly improved your lead time by reducing the seven wastes.
2. The future state provides a starting point for "backward planning," a time-tested technique for strategic planning that uses the ideal state as a starting point for building a better future.
3. It dislodges even stubborn holdouts on the team from old patterns of thinking about their organization and their respective roles in it.

In the ideal future state, the patient never has to wait for service, and clinical processes flow without interruption. For example, because time is of the essence for a patient in trauma, the patient flows through a carefully organized process that involves all clinicians and support staff simultaneously in one space. As we will see in Chapter 5, the same type of flow can often be established in other healthcare contexts by systematically eliminating delays and other of the seven wastes.

Frequently, though, it is impossible or too costly to eliminate all delays and other wastes because of architectural constraints or because of the sheer variability in certain healthcare subprocesses. In such cases, it is important to link the "islands of flow" together with a *pull system.*

Definition

A pull system is a system of carefully balanced schedules and buffer stocks of resources (mainly staffed and stocked beds and exam rooms) that can absorb the variation in either the demand for or supply of healthcare services that otherwise might disrupt the flow. We will see several examples of a pull system in healthcare in Chapter 6.

3.7 USING VALUE STREAM MAPPING ICONS

New Tool

As you read Chapters 4, 5, and 6, you will be introduced to the visual language of value stream mapping, which utilizes a standard set of so-called "icons." Icons fall into two broad categories: patient flow icons and information flow icons. Additional, more general icons will be introduced later. The 11 most commonly used icons include:

Icon	Name	Description
Operation	Process	Indicates an area of flow in the healthcare value stream. *Note: This icon is also used to represent the patient, as well as for scheduling and other types of departmental processes.*
(data box)	Data box	Records critical information about the patient, a healthcare operation, department, etc.
(triangle)	Wait	Indicates points in the process of care where patients wait an unspecified amount of time for service.
(striped arrow)	Push	Indicates that patients are served and moved to the next operation in the process before that operation is ready to provide care.
FIFO	FIFO lane	Indicates the transfer of controlled numbers of patients in a first-in/first-out (FIFO) sequence. *Note: In a FIFO lane, patients wait no longer than X.*
(curved arrow)	Withdrawal	Indicates the pull of patients from upstream operations by downstream operations that are ready to provide service. *Note: Patients are normally pulled from buffers attached to the providing upstream operation.*
(buffer bracket)	Buffer	Indicates a buffer of appropriately staffed and stocked rooms, beds, or other venues of care where patients wait a predetermined amount of time before being pulled by downstream operations. *Note: This icon always appears with the withdrawal icon.*
→	Verbal or manual information	Indicates a verbal or manual instruction for a healthcare operation to produce a service for the patient.
(zigzag arrow)	Electronic information	Indicates an electronic instruction for a healthcare operation to produce a service for the patient.
Daily Schedule	Schedule	Indicates a schedule to produce healthcare services that involve the physical presence of the patient.
O X O X	Level loading	Indicates reprioritization of patient flow based upon the acuity of the patient's condition or a constraint in the process. *Note: This icon always appears with the buffer icon.*

3.8 SUMMARY

A *value stream* is a collection or set of processes and operations—together with their constituent skilled people, methods, materials, medication, and equipment—required to provide a well-defined family of deliverables.

Value stream mapping helps us visualize an entire flow of service production and delivery from beginning to end. Healthcare organizations often organize their clinical processes into organizational divisions known as "service lines." This is very often a good place to start with value stream mapping.

The purpose of value stream mapping is first to identify and then to remove all non-value-added activity (waste) from a process. *Value* is the price a person is willing to pay in exchange for a good or service. A caregiving activity is *value added* if it changes the course of the patient's disease process in a way that is helpful to the patient's recovery or if it improves the patient's comfort and sense of well-being. *Waste* is anything that does not add value to the process of creating or delivering a healthcare service.

There are the four basic steps in creating a value stream map:

1. Define the value that the process delivers to the patient by specifying a *service family*. A *service family* is a set of healthcare services that tend to consume a similar constellation of resources: skilled clinicians, medication, equipment, physical spaces, etc.
2. Build and analyze a *current-state map*. *A current-state map describes the essential operations of a healthcare process as they currently are practiced; the map is then used to identify systematically which activities are value added and which are waste.*
3. Brainstorm and build a *future-state map* that establishes flow wherever possible and—where flow is not possible—links islands of flow together with a *pull system*. A *pull system* is a system of carefully balanced schedules and buffer stocks of resources (mainly staffed and stocked beds and exam rooms) that can absorb the variation in either the demand for or supply of healthcare services that otherwise might disrupt the flow.
4. Implement and perfect improvements.

The visual language of value stream mapping utilizes a standard set of icons. The 11 most commonly used icons fall into two broad categories: patient flow icons and information flow icons.

3.9 REFLECTIONS

Now that you have completed this chapter, take 5 minutes to think about these questions and write down your answers:

- What did you learn from reading this chapter that stands out as being particularly useful or interesting to you in healthcare?
- Do you have any questions about the topics presented in this chapter? If so, what are they?

- How do you feel about mapping the patient's experience in traveling through current-state value streams with which you are involved?
- Are there any special obstacles in your mind or the minds of your colleagues to mapping either the operations or process of healthcare?
- What information do you still need to understand fully the ideas presented?
- How can you get this information?
- Whom do you need to involve in this process?

Chapter 4

Map the Current State

4.1 THE POWER OF DIRECT OBSERVATION

Key Point

Most clinicians spend their time concentrating on only one operation in the process of delivering healthcare: the operation for which they are expertly qualified and licensed to practice. Many healthcare executives concentrate on attending meetings and reading abstract reports, rather than on observing the processes of healthcare as they unfold from day to day. *Frequently, it is only the patient who actually sees what is happening throughout the value stream.* The empirical method of value stream mapping changes all of this and permits us to pursue genuinely patient-centered care.

The purpose of current-state mapping is to observe the process from the patient's point of view—as it actually occurs—and to record vital process statistics. When you implement improvements (which we will explore in Chapter 5), these statistics become the basis of in-process measures of productivity and quality that help clinicians synchronize their delivery of safe, high-quality healthcare services.

Definition

The Japanese call this method of observation *genchi genbutsu. Genchi genbutsu means "go see for yourself what is really happening."* This is empirical science, pure and simple. Think of Leonardo da Vinci's famous dissections, conducted while he was an intern at the famous hospital, Santa Maria Nuova, in Florence, Italy. Leonardo did not rely upon ancient manuscripts recently translated from Arabic and Greek; he went to see for himself how the human body was put together and how it functioned. The result was his series of exquisite drawings of the human body and the beginning of the modern science of anatomy. Likewise, we must abandon the normal constraints of our managerial and clinical specialties and walk with the patient to see, perhaps for the first time, how the tasks, operations, and processes of healthcare are put together and how they really function—from the patient's perspective. The result will be a series of value stream maps that represent a point of departure for the future of healthcare.

4.2 BUILDING A CURRENT-STATE MAP

How-to Steps

There are 10 steps to observing processes and building a current-state map that faithfully records our observations. Each step listed in Figure 4.1 is described in detail later. Before you begin mapping, we recommend that you reserve a meeting room in which to build your map. You will need a space big enough to train your team and conduct conversations once you return from observing the actual area where the work is performed (or, the "gemba," as it is commonly referred to in Lean management, which is the Japanese word for "the real place").

Some people prefer to use sticky notes to build their maps, in which case you will need at least 20 feet of free wall space and either rolls of butcher paper or sticky-backed poster paper (the latter is more flexible and easier to transport to your final report out). Other people prefer to use paper and pencil; in this case, provide multiple sheets of tabloid size (11 × 17 inches) paper, no. 2 pencils, erasers, and plenty of room to draw.

Value stream maps are often constructed by small teams of three or four people, but we recommend fielding a team of 12 to 15 members. True value streams often span multiple service lines, departments, and locations. A larger number of team members will permit the workshop leader to organize the team into four or five small groups that can collect data on multiple gembas during a single week.

Most of your team members should be drawn from the processes and operations that make up the service family being mapped. They will know the clinical subject matter as well as the organizational history behind the current practice. You should also include at least two pairs of "outside eyes"—that is, team members who are *not* familiar with the process. They will ask questions about current practice that will not occur to team members who have become habituated to the status quo. Patients are also excellent participants on your value stream mapping team. It is often a revelation for clinicians and healthcare executives to hear patients tell their stories of what really happens during and between healthcare process steps.

---

1. Choose a service family.
2. Identify the patient.
3. Walk the value stream and gather data.
4. Identify sequential operations in the process.
5. Identify operational metrics.
6. Identify waits between operations.
7. Document how work is prioritized.
8. Identify manual and electronic information flows.
9. Identify external patient flows.
10. Build a process time line and calculate summary statistics.

Figure 4.1 Ten steps for building a current-state map.

For more pointers on how to prepare for and conduct team-based improvement activities, see *Kaizen Workshops for Lean Healthcare* (T. L. Jackson, editor, New York: Productivity Press, 2012).

4.2.1 Choose a Service Family

Key Point
As covered in Chapter 3, a service family is a set of services that consumes a similar constellation of resources, including skilled clinicians, medicines, medical equipment, physical spaces, etc. *A simple way to identify potential service families is to analyze the resources typically used in providing different services.*

Figure 4.2 shows an analysis of the resource-consumption pattern of different diagnoses or case types in the emergency room. Two service families emerge from the analysis. The first is the family of acute emergency cases (diagnoses C, D, G, and H). These cases frequently require clinical resources to stabilize the patient, often result in a hospital stay, and require significant diagnostic work prior to treatment or admission to the hospital. The second is the family of relatively nonacute cases (diagnoses A, B, E, and F). These cases do not often require clinicians to stabilize the patient and usually result in some minor treatment, after which the patient may go home. Diagnostic work by ancillary processes is often not involved. The main example in this book follows an acutely ill patient from arrival in the emergency department to admission to the hospital.

Key Point
By choosing a service family, we narrow the scope of observation by focusing on a set of processes and constituent human and material resources that should benefit from being administered as a single system. *More often than not, both cost and quality can be substantially improved by locating related processes and resources more closely together or even in the same place.* Sorting processes and resources administratively and physically into well-organized

| | | Emergency Clinical Staff, Operations, and Equipment | | | | | | | |
		Nurse	Doctor	Multiple doctors	E.D. tech	Simple blood work	Complex blood work	X-ray	E.D. procedure	CAT scan
Diagnosis	A. Simple wrist fracture	X	X		X			X	X	
	B. Bronchitis	X	X		X	X		X		
	C. Diverticulitis	X	X		X	X	X	X		X
	D. Stroke	X	X		X	X	X			X
	E. Acute otitis media	X	X		X					
	F. Tonsillitis, uncomplicated	X	X		X	X				
	G. Multiple trauma	X	X	X	X	X	X	X	X	X
	H. Pneumonia with effusion	X	X		X	X	X	X	X	X

Figure 4.2 Process capacity table.

value streams can directly reduce the variation in healthcare that creates delays and defects. In the case of the emergency department, although acute and nonacute cases share important resources, they follow different paths and behave according to different rules that we will explore in Chapters 5 and 6.

Take Five

Take 5 minutes to think about these questions and to write down your answers:

1. What is the purpose of building a current-state map?
2. How would you begin to identify a service family in your health-care facility?
3. Who do you think would be good candidates for participating in a value stream mapping project in your area?

4.2.2 Identify the Patient

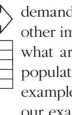

How-to Steps

To start your value stream map, draw the patient-as-customer icon, to identify the patient, in the upper right-hand corner of your map.

Underneath the customer icon, draw a data box and record the average demand for the services being mapped, hours open for services, and any other important statistics about patient demand. (See Figure 4.3.) For instance, what are the distinguishing characteristics of the patient population? Is the population defined by geography (for example, city or county), by age (for example, pediatric or geriatric), or by diagnosis (for example, diabetes)? In our example, the average daily demand is 100 patients per day. Of these 100 patients, 33%, or 33 patients, are expected to be admitted to the hospital. The time available to produce healthcare services is 24 hours a day (over two

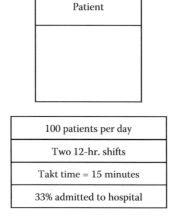

Figure 4.3 Who is the customer?

12-hour shifts). The "takt time" is 15 minutes. (Takt time is a useful measure that will help you match the pace of healthcare service production to daily demand; it will be covered in more detail in Chapter 5.)

4.2.3 Walk the Value Stream and Gather Data

Now it is time to follow Leonardo da Vinci's example and "go see" the service family you have chosen. Before your value stream mapping workshop, walk the value stream. This means beginning where the patient will begin his journey and tracing his path to wellness. If you know approximately where the patient lives, try to experience the modes of transportation that the patient will use to travel to all the venues of care. If the patient has scheduled an appointment with his primary care physician, visit his outpatient clinic; sit in the waiting room, and walk to registration, to the exam room, and out the door again. If the physician has scheduled surgery, drive to the hospital and visit the operating room. If the patient will be admitted to the hospital for postoperative care, visit the nursing floor. During the workshop, divide the team into subteams and ask them to visit all of these gembas to make and record observations.

Key Point

Whether before or during the workshop, by yourself or in a group, when you arrive at the workplace, set the stage by explaining to the frontline caregivers what you wish to do and what you expect to accomplish. Of course, you must also ask the permission of any patients that you wish to follow. (In my experience, patients rarely refuse.) Always express respect for the patient. Unless you are following a clinician or support staff member, it is not often necessary to enter the room in which patient care is being delivered.

If you plan to follow patients, it is important to be prepared to wait. Despite the best laid plans, in healthcare observers may often feel like surfers waiting to catch a wave. Even in scheduled healthcare operations—for example, in the outpatient clinic setting—patient arrivals can be "catch as catch can." This is certainly true in the setting of emergent care, where patient arrivals are not scheduled at all. Coordinate your visits with the manager of the area you wish to observe. Check the schedule the day before you go to learn how many patients in your service family have been scheduled and at what times. During the workshop, plan to check the schedule frequently to maximize the utilization of the team.

New Tool

Definition

When it is time to go, you must be ready with two tools: (1) time observation forms and (2) standard work sheets.

The time observation form documents observations of the elapsed time of a patient visit from the perspectives of the patient and the attending clinicians. (See Figure 4.4.) The time observation form is used to list the sequential work tasks in an operation, as experienced from the patient's perspective (when we are following the patient) or from the clinician's perspective (when we are following a clinician). The elapsed time that appears on the stopwatch at the

Rona consulting group

Area/location: **emergency department**						Date of observation: **December 31, 2009**	
Subject observed: **patient**						Start time: **11:30 pm**	
Process: **door to doc**						Observer: **Nancy**	

Step no.	Description of operation	Observation time					Mode (most freq. occurring) task time	Remarks
		Observations						
		1	2	3	4	5		
1	Greet	0 / 3:30	0:00 / 3:00	0:00 / 4:00	—	—	3:30	
2	Wait	3:30 / 5:00	3:00 / 5:30	4:00 / 2:00	—	—	5:00	
3	Triage	8:30 / 7:00	8:30 / 8:30	6:00 / 3:00	—	—	7:00	**3rd patient had chest pain**
4	Wait	15:30 / 5:00	17:00 / 4:00	9:00 / 1:00	—	—	4:00	
5		20:30	21:00	10:00				

Figure 4.4 Time observation form.

beginning of each task is recorded in the upper box next to each task, and later the "element time" (or total time consumed by each component task) is recorded in the lower box next to each task.

Definition

The standard work sheet documents the flow of the clinicians, capturing their movement through the physical environment in which the caregiving process occurs. (See Figure 4.5.) For more information about how to use time observation forms and standard work sheets, see *Standard Work for Healthcare* (T. L. Jackson, editor, New York: Productivity Press, 2011), another book in the Lean Tools for Healthcare series.

Chart Review

There are many situations in which it is impractical to follow the patient. For example, it is impractical to follow a single patient through a trip to the emergency department, then to surgery, and then through an extended stay in the hospital, or to follow a single patient from a visit to his primary care physician and then to surgery, say, 4 months later. In such situations, chart review is an acceptable proxy to firsthand observation.

Chart review is not, however, the best approach to value stream mapping. When chart review must be employed, it is vital to supplement it with as many firsthand observations as you can obtain. Let us assume that you have chart review data for a single patient who has visited the emergency department, surgery, and the hospital. In such a case, supplement the chart review with direct observations of

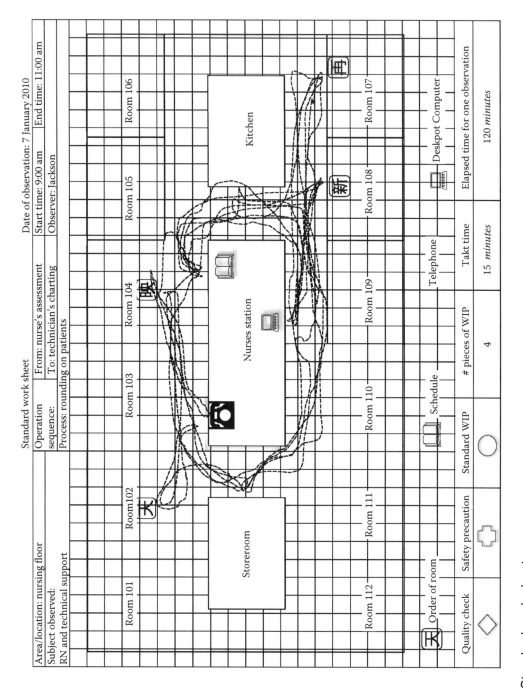

Figure 4.5 Standard work sheet.

similar patients in all three settings. Such observations should be easily obtainable during the 5 days of a value stream mapping workshop.

When necessary, a sample of five patients should be sufficient; a larger sample is always better. Direct observations are always the best, but if you have trouble finding enough patients to follow, consider using chart reviews to supplement your team's direct observations. You may validate your wait times, cycle times, and setup times by conducting chart reviews of representative cases. Be careful, however, because the data entered in the chart are not normally gathered by people trained in value stream mapping. Also, there are frequently delays between the delivery and the charting of care, and charting errors can creep into records. Nevertheless, such data can be very useful to confirm your time studies or to substitute for them when they are not feasible.

4.2.4 Identify Sequential Operations in the Process

How-to Steps

Operation

With the information you have gathered using standard work sheets and time observation forms, you may now begin to build your value stream map. Draw a process box icon to record each operation in the process that you observed in gemba. *Remember:* an operation is a repeating cycle of tasks; in contrast, a process can combine one or more operations to achieve flow.

Background

INFO

In manufacturing, the scientific observation of process has been going on for more than 100 years; healthcare is really just getting started. We know a lot about the individual operations—the procedures and protocols—of healthcare. We know very little about healthcare process (i.e., the sequence and timing of operations). (This may be why it is in the hand-offs between operations where most of the defects in healthcare occur.) Value stream mapping presents us with a major opportunity to observe and record—frequently for the first time—the sequence and timing of healthcare operations. Meanwhile, the language of value stream mapping allows us to begin at the level of operations and step up to the level of process and value stream. In Chapter 5, we will see how to combine and colocate individual operations into efficient, defect-free processes. In Chapter 6, we will see how to link processes into value streams.

Key Point

The value stream map should record operations in the sequence that they normally occur (i.e., 60% to 80% of the time). Ignore all of the workarounds that you will surely observe. Workarounds are normally idiomatic—that is, specific to certain clinicians or staff members, as in, "Oh, that's the way that Dr. So-and-So deals with that situation." Workarounds—which abound in healthcare—should *not* be mapped as part of the value stream but rather treated as process defects. Defects should be mapped separately as part of a defect reduction project using a method such as mistake proofing. See *Mistake Proofing for Lean Healthcare* (T. L. Jackson, editor, New York: Productivity Press, 2013). Do, however, map every normally occurring or "cyclical" operation, regardless of whether or not it will be proved later to add value.

4.2.5 Identify Operational Metrics

How-to Steps

Definition

For each operation you identify in the process, draw a data box to record essential information about the operation and post these data underneath their corresponding activity boxes on your value stream map. (See Figure 4.6.) The minimum statistics for the data box include *cycle time, value-added time, and non-value-added time.*

Cycle time is the time it normally takes a clinician to complete all of the work of giving care before repeating the operation for the next patient. It is also how often we should expect to see a patient exiting an operation in the process.

Value-added time is the time of those component tasks recorded on the time observation form that actually change or transform the patient's condition in a way that the patient would be willing to pay for, normally through diagnosis, pain control, and treatment.

The difference between the cycle time and the value-added time is called *non-value-added time*—that is, the time of component tasks recorded on the time observation form that fall into one of several categories of six of the seven wastes: waiting, defects or rework, transport, motion, overprocessing, or overproduction. The seventh waste, inventory, is the subject of *Kanban for Lean Healthcare* (T. L. Jackson, editor, New York: Productivity Press, 2013).

In the case of an operation that serves a diverse product family, you may wish to record the typical setup time—that is, the time it takes to get ready

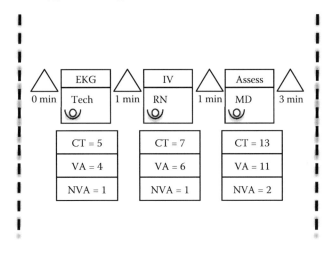

Figure 4.6 Activities, waits, and process measures.

for the next process. If the operation is subject to significant defects, you may also wish to record the defect rate, if known.

4.2.6 Identify Waits between Operations

Definition

Use the triangular "wait" icon to identify where patients wait between operations in the process, as shown in Figure 4.6. On the triangle, record the observed *wait time. Wait time is the most commonly recurring elapsed time between the completion of one cycle of work (an operation or a process) and the beginning of another cycle of work.*

What the triangle icon really represents is an unmanaged line or "queue." Within the queue, it is not obvious to the patient how long the wait will be or even the order in which she and other patients will be processed. The wait time and the order of processing are not necessarily clear to clinicians either! In Chapters 5 and 6, we will see how to eliminate or at least regulate the waits between operations and processes.

How to Handle In-Cycle Waits

On the time observation form, you certainly will have recorded several wait times *within* the cycle of work. Treat these waits as elements of the operation in the current state. In-cycle waits should not be counted as wait times on the triangles on the value stream map. These wait times are accounted for when you calculate your non-value-added time for the work cycle.

4.2.7 Document How Work Is Prioritized

Key Point

Use the appropriate work prioritization icons to identify the methods by which process managers and clinicians decide to advance patients through the healthcare process. *There are two basic methods and corresponding icons: "push" and "pull."*

The first method of work prioritization is the method of "push." The icon for push is a cross-hatched arrow. In healthcare today, patients normally proceed from one operation to the next without regard to the readiness of the downstream operation. Patients wait in waiting rooms and exam rooms because clinicians are not ready to see them. Patients wait on gurneys in emergency room hallways because clinicians have not discharged patients who are ready to leave. Use the push arrow icon to indicate that the patient moves from the

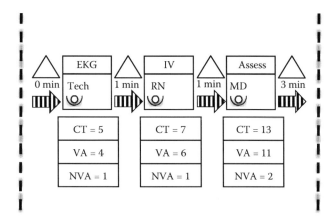

Figure 4.7   How is work prioritized?

upstream operation to the downstream operation before that operation is ready. (See Figure 4.7.) Most healthcare operations are "push."

In Chapter 5, we will learn a second method, called "pull," for clinicians to prioritize work as it moves from one operation to the next. The icon for pull is called a "withdrawal icon," represented by an arrow that spirals counterclockwise. Patients (patients as inputs, that is) can be "pulled" through the process by demand signals generated by the downstream operation (i.e., the next operation in the process). In such cases, we will use a pull icon on the value stream map.

At this point, we have mapped the entire current-state process from beginning to end, including basic activities, wait times, process measures, and method of prioritization (in this case, "push"). The complete process portion of the map is shown in Figure 4.8.

Take Five

Take 5 minutes to think about these questions and to write down your answers:

1. Where would you go to get information on typical demand in a service family in which you participate?
2. If a team were coming to observe work and map the value stream in your area, what information would you like to be communicated in advance?
3. How would you conduct time observations in your own area?
4. Can you think of any areas in which work is *not* prioritized by "push"?

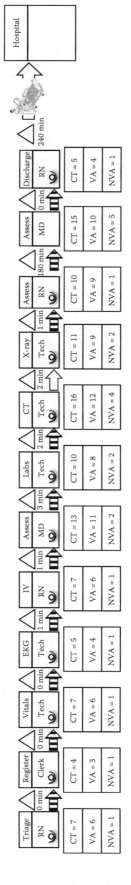

Figure 4.8 The process from beginning to end.

4.2.8 Identify Manual and Electronic Information Flows

Next we must identify the flows of information that trigger the movement of the patient or production of healthcare services.

Use the verbal/manual information icon to indicate that information is transmitted verbally or manually. For example, in an emergency room or on a nursing floor, instructions to room or discharge patients are frequently communicated verbally by a charge nurse. Instructions to conduct tests or to treat patients may be made in writing by physicians. In such cases, use the verbal/manual information icon.

Use the "lightning bolt" icon to indicate that instructions are communicated by telephone, e-mail, fax, or another electronic signal.

Too Many Information Systems to Map?

New Tool

Mapping the flow of information with electronic and manual icons in healthcare can often lead to confusion, either because you have not converted to electronic medical records (EMRs) and there are many physical hand-offs of information or because you have not completed your conversion and there are manual as well as electronic hand-offs for which to account. Or perhaps you have already converted to EMR but you still have multiple electronic systems for different functions: emergency room, hospital, case management, public health, and so on.

In such cases, we recommend using a *standard work sheet* to document your many hand-offs. (See Figure 4.9.)

4.2.9 Identify External Patient Flows

The movement of the patient to and from the clinic or emergency room or hospital normally happens in several ways. If the person is ambulatory, use the transport arrow icon and the car or public transport icons to indicate that the patient moves herself. If the person is not ambulatory, use the transport arrow icon and the ambulance icon. The current-state map with information flows and external patient flows is shown in Figure 4.10.

4.2.10 Build a Process Time Line and Calculate Summary Statistics

As illustrated in Figure 4.11, draw a time line or "castle wall" underneath your value stream map. The openings in the wall should line up with your activity boxes. Now transpose the wait time in the triangles to the corresponding

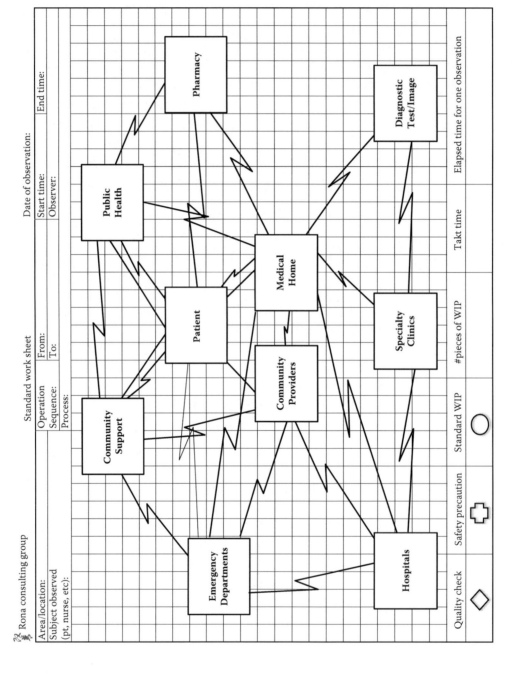

Figure 4.9 Mapping complex information flows.

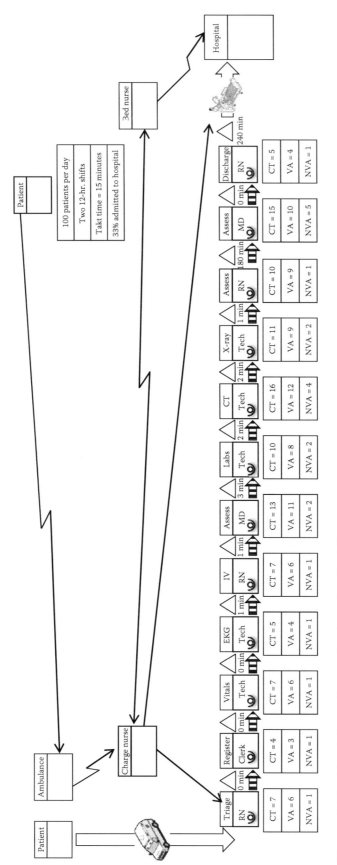

Figure 4.10 Map information and external patient flows.

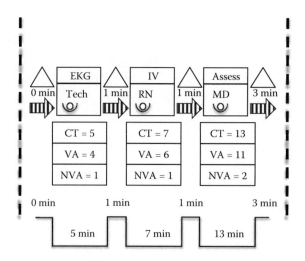

Figure 4.11   Build a "castle wall."

"crenulations" or high points in the wall and the cycle times in the activity boxes to the openings or low points in the wall.

Definition

Finally, calculate the process lead time. *Lead time is the time it takes a single patient to move all the way through a process or an entire value stream from start to finish.* Lead time is calculated by summing all cycle times and all wait times and then adding these two sums together. The summary data box is shown at the far right of Figure 4.12, in the completed acute emergency care current-state map.

$$LT = CT + WT = 110 \text{ minutes} + 430 \text{ minutes} = 540 \text{ minutes}$$

In this instance, the lead time is the total time that the patient spent in the emergency department until she was transferred to the hospital.

Definition

Next, sum all the value-added times in all the activity boxes. Finally, divide the total value-added time by the total lead time to create a *value-added ratio*. *The value-added ratio is the percent of time in a process or value stream that the patient receives valuable services; the rest is waste.* This is shown in the completed current-state map in Figure 4.12.

$$VAR = VA/LT = 88 \text{ minutes}/540 \text{ minutes} = 16\%$$

4.3 ANOTHER EXAMPLE

Example

In Figure 4.12 we saw an example based upon our decision to follow a highly acute patient through the emergency department. In Figure 4.13 we see a value stream map constructed for a nonacute patient's trip through the "ready care" area of the same emergency department.

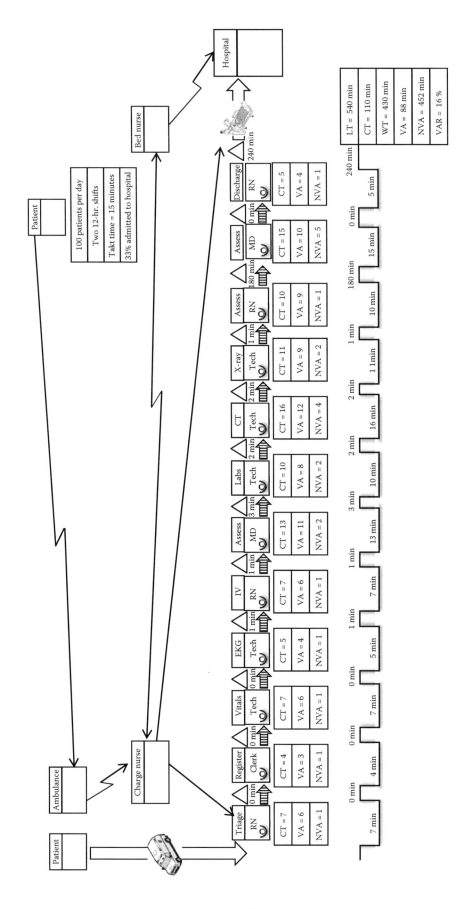

Figure 4.12 Completed acute emergency care current-state map.

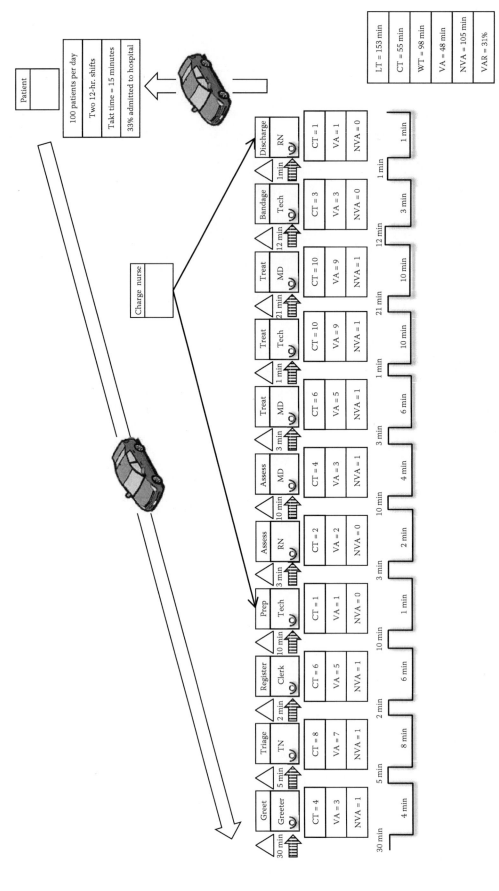

Figure 4.13 Ready-care current-state map.

A number of distinctions are evident. First, we see that this patient had to wait 30 minutes before being triaged. Second, the patient did not require several operations, including EKG, IV, and imaging. Third, the patient did not wait for hours at the end of the value stream to be admitted to the hospital. At the far right of Figure 4.13 we see the summary data box for the ready-care current-state map:

$$LT = CT + WT = 55 \text{ minutes} + 98 \text{ minutes} = 153 \text{ minutes}$$

$$VAR = VA/LT = 48 \text{ minutes}/153 \text{ minutes} = 31\%$$

4.4 SUMMARY

Value stream mapping begins with the direct observation of healthcare operations and processes. It is difficult to underestimate the power of direct observation in healthcare. Beginning with the observations of the human body made by Leonardo da Vinci, it is one of the pillars of modern medicine and healthcare.

A little preparation is required before you take your team to the gemba (i.e., the actual place where healthcare services are delivered to the patient). To orient yourself to the value stream prior to your value stream mapping workshop, plan to walk the path of the patient through multiple gembas, if necessary. Coordinate with area managers to let them know that you are coming. Before and during the workshop, monitor patient schedules so that you can match your team's resources with opportunities to observe the process.

On the gemba, carefully observe and record healthcare operations using standard work sheets and time observation forms. Healthcare is in its industrial infancy. Although we know a lot about individual procedures and protocols (the operations), we know little about their timing and sequence (the process). Meanwhile, the procedures and protocols are often not standard among clinicians. Value stream mapping represents a major opportunity to record for the first time what actually happens to a patient once he or she signs a consent form. When we introduce future-state mapping in Chapters 5 and 6, we will see how to standardize and combine operations into efficient processes and value streams. Our ability to envision the future, however, will depend upon how closely we have observed and recorded the details of actual practice in our current-state map.

4.5 REFLECTIONS

Now that you have completed this chapter, take 5 minutes to think about these questions and write down your answers:

- What did you learn from reading this chapter that stands out as being particularly useful or interesting to you in healthcare?
- How do you feel about the idea of "mapping" healthcare services using industrial methods?
- Do you have any questions about the topics presented in this chapter? If so, what are they?
- Are there any special obstacles in your mind or the minds of your colleagues to mapping either the operations or process of healthcare?
- What information do you still need to understand fully the ideas presented?
- How can you get this information?
- Whom do you need to involve in this process?

Chapter 5

Map the Future State: Phase I—Flow

5.1 PRINCIPLES OF FLOW PRODUCTION IN HEALTHCARE

How-to Steps

As we saw in Chapter 2, the third principle of Lean management is flow production, and that is what future-state maps are designed to help us envision and create. The discipline of future-state mapping employs six guidelines in order to accomplish two things: (1) imagine new processes that establish flow wherever possible and (2) protect that flow by using pull systems and buffers of appropriately staffed rooms and beds where flow is not yet practical. (See Figure 5.1.) Thus, future-state mapping falls naturally into two distinct phases: flow and pull.

OVERVIEW

This chapter covers phase I of future-state mapping, which is defined by guidelines one and two of the future-state mapping process outlined in Figure 5.1: produce to takt time and flow the process. These two guidelines focus on creating an ideal state of smooth production flow capable of meeting our patients' demand for healthcare services. In Chapter 6, we will explore phase II of future-state mapping, which is defined by guidelines three through six. These guidelines explain how to build future-state maps when we have exhausted opportunities to create flow and must manage processes according to *pull*. Whenever we cannot flow, rather than push patients to the next operation in the process, we will learn to buffer the flow with appropriately staffed beds and other venues of care, where patients will be asked to wait a short time while the caregiving activities for the preceding patient are completed.

The concept of flow helps us to think about sources of variation in our process that might be eliminated. Conceptually, flow is what happens when the seven deadly wastes have been eradicated from a process. Think of a river with no rocks to obstruct the movement of water, no zigzags in the course of the river, and no logs or other flotsam and jetsam to disturb the water's surface.

To many clinicians, the concept of flow may at first seem counterintuitive and even counter to patient safety. "Patients are not cars,"

1. Produce to takt time.	Synchronize the pace of service production across all operations in your healthcare processes by carefully pacing production at each operation to meet your expected daily demand.
2. Flow the process.	Ideally, serve patients one at a time and hand each patient immediately, in order, from one clinical operation to the next within healthcare production "cells."
3. If you cannot flow, pull.	Where patients cannot be served one at a time because of their medical condition, or where production gets backed up and patients wait because of process constraints, "pull" the patient to the downstream process from first-in/first-out lanes and/or "buffers" of appropriately staffed venues of care, but only when that process is ready to produce the service required.
4. Pull to the pacemaker.	Send the patient schedule to only one operation—known as the *pacemaker*—in the process; then, pull the patient from upstream processes to the pacemaker.
5. Level the volume.	To avoid amplifying variability in the upstream pace of production, order small, consistent bundles of healthcare services at the pacemaker.
6. Level the case mix.	To improve the synchronization of production throughout the value stream, at the pacemaker, distribute the production of different healthcare services (diagnoses, acuity levels, etc.) evenly over time.

Figure 5.1   Six guidelines of future-state mapping.

it is often said, and that is true. Flow appears to require patients to behave as if they were parts on an assembly line. Obviously, flow is not always possible or even desirable in healthcare because patients (1) sometimes require a process step that keeps them from "flowing" and (2) sometimes step "out of line" as a result of their medical condition. When flow is correctly understood, however, it becomes clear that by promoting and protecting flow, clinicians can more effectively serve even the sickest and most unpredictable of patients. In Chapter 6, we will see that even when patients cannot or should not flow, the concept can help create better-managed healthcare processes that ensure patient safety and good clinical outcomes.

5.2 BUILDING A FUTURE-STATE MAP WITH FLOW

In building a current-state value stream map, you have already

1. Chosen a service family
2. Identified the patient
3. Walked the value stream and gathered data
4. Identified sequential operations in the process
5. Identified operational metrics
6. Identified waits between operations
7. Documented how work is prioritized
8. Identified manual and electronic information flows
9. Identified external patient flows
10. Built a process time line and calculated summary statistics

In phase I of future-state mapping, you will revisit your current-state map and do two things:

How-to Steps

1. Produce services to takt time.
2. Eliminate unnecessary waits and create clinical cells.

Take Five

Take 5 minutes to think about these questions and to write down your answers:

1. What are the two phases of future-state mapping?
2. What benefits do you think would come from establishing flow in your area?

5.2.1 Produce Services to Takt Time

Principle

Synchronize the pace of service production across all operations in your healthcare processes by carefully pacing production at each operation according to your expected daily demand.

Definition

A Lean healthcare value stream produces healthcare services according to *takt time. Takt time is a measure of the pace of your expected production that provides a baseline for adjusting staffing and other resource allocation decisions as actual demand fluctuates from expected demand.* Takt time is also an in-process measure of efficiency. When coupled with the in-process quality measures of autonomation discussed in Chapter 2, it produces a powerful one–two punch that effectively tackles the problems of quality and cost in healthcare.

Clinicians normally measure the number of patients seen in a day or a shift. This is an *outcome* measure, and it makes sense only at the end of the time period (at the end of the day or shift) for which output (patients seen) is being measured. Outcome measures answer the question: *How did we do?* The purpose of takt time is to focus our attention on the *process* instead of on *outcomes*. Takt time asks the question: *How are we doing right now?* Takt time is a calculated number that measures the pulse of market demand for healthcare services.

The basic takt time formula is as follows:

$$\text{Takt time} = \text{net available time/average demand}$$

Definition

Available time is the time scheduled for the delivery of healthcare services. Net available time is the time scheduled for the delivery of healthcare services, less time scheduled for lunches, dinners, breaks, and meetings (if the operation is closed to patients during those times). If you plan to stagger lunches, dinners, and breaks (as is common in many healthcare operations), do not deduct time for these because service is continuous. If you deduct staggered times, it will throw off your staffing calculations.

Definition

Average demand is the mean of your historical demand for the period (a day, a shift, etc.) for which you are calculating takt time.

New Tool

You may use the work sheet in Figure 5.2 to calculate takt time for a service or service family. In this example, which is based upon the emergency department introduced in Chapter 4, the patients arriving at the emergency department represent two different service families: (a) highly acute patients needing emergency care and (b) relatively nonacute patients requiring what has become known as "ready" or "fast track" care. In Chapter 5, we will follow the service family of ready care.

Example

Because the ready-care facility is open from 8:00 a.m. to 8:00 p.m., the scheduled "available" time is 12 hours. All breaks and lunches are staggered, so no deductions are required and the "net available time" is also 12 hours or 720 minutes. As we learned in Chapter 4, on average, 100 patients arrive at our emergency department every day, and 33% of these patients will normally be admitted to the hospital. This means that, on average, 67%, or 64 patients, will be treated and discharged home. The takt time for ready care is thus 12 hours or 720 minutes divided by 64 patients, or 11.25 minutes. In other words, if we were to sit in the medical center parking lot during the hours of 8:00 a.m. to 8:00 p.m., we should expect to see a patient exit the ready-care facility every 11.25 minutes—*assuming,* of course, that the fast track is capable of meeting takt time.

Takt time calculation		No. shifts/day	1
	×	No. hours/shift	× 12
Available time	=	**No. hours/day**	**12**
	×	60 minutes/hour	× 60
	=	No. minutes/day	720
	−	Breaks (minutes)[a]	0
	−	Lunch (minutes)[a]	0
	−	Setup (minutes)[a]	0
	−	Other (minutes)[a]	0
Net available time	=	**Total minutes**	**720**
	÷	Patients/day	÷ 64
Takt time	=	**Minutes**	**11.25**
[a] Include only if operation is closed for business during this time.			

Figure 5.2 Takt time calculation.

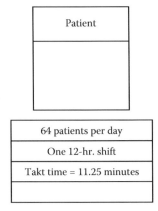

Figure 5.3 Ready-care patient profile.

We begin building our future-state map by posting the patient icon with a data box below it reporting the information about our ready-care service family. (See Figure 5.3.) It is important to note that this takt time does not mean that the patient encounter will take 11.25 minutes; it is simply the rate at which patients must move, on average, from one process to the next.

To some, calculating a separate takt time for ready-care patients may seem to omit our sicker acute patients, whom we may actually see under the same roof! We have not forgotten that acute patients require special treatment. We will revisit acute care in Chapter 6 when we look at pull systems.

5.2.2 Eliminate Waits to Flow the Process

Principle

Ideally, serve patients one at a time, and hand each patient immediately, in order, from one clinical operation to the next.

In a Lean healthcare value stream, *continuous flow* has been developed wherever it is possible. Continuous flow means serving one patient at a time, passing each patient from one operation in the process to the next without waiting (or other types of non-value-added waste) between operations. Again, it is useful to think of flow as an ideal state or antichaos principle. In the first phase of planning a future state, we identify opportunities to flow the process by eliminating waits and other easily corrected wastes such as unnecessary walking and transportation. Another way to put this is that in phase I of future-state mapping, we harvest the "low-hanging fruit" of opportunity. The objective is to create better flow wherever we can.

Use the process box icon to indicate flow within a process or operation. When you build your future-state map, each activity box will describe an area of flow, just as it did in the current-state maps in Chapter 4. In the current state, however, many operations are frequently interrupted by unmanaged waits (represented on the current-state map by the triangular wait icon) and patients moving to the head of the line because of their medical condition.

5.2.3 Create Continuous Flow with Clinical Cells

Continuous flow production is the production of healthcare services to patients in a first-in/first-out order with zero waits between tasks and operations in the process. As a practical matter, this means that you should try to eliminate as many waits (triangles) as possible between operations on your current-state map (see Figure 5.4). When a new operation that results from combining several old operations is designed to perform to takt time, the outcome is called a *clinical cell*.

A clinical cell is an arrangement of clinical staff, equipment, medicines, and supplies (in a single space) with the capability of producing healthcare services for patients—at takt time—without waiting periods between the various tasks and hand-offs that define the operation. The icon used to denote a cell contains an upside-down "U" and symbols that stand for three staff members (or operators).

An example of a healthcare cell is the operating room, where physicians and nurses work in close physical proximity as a team. Continuous flow through cellular production can often be created in other areas of healthcare by using the five basic steps of **F-E-C-R-S:**

1. **F**ix broken operations.
2. **E**liminate unnecessary waits and operations.
3. **C**ombine or colocate operations, clinicians, equipment, space, etc.
4. **R**earrange operations.
5. **S**tandardize and simplify operations.

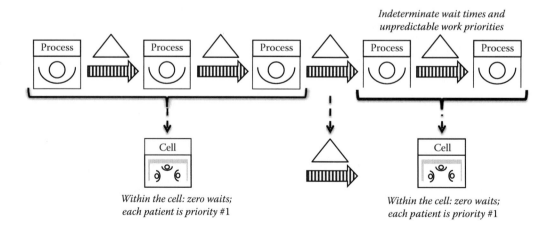

Figure 5.4 Creating continuous flow in clinical cells.

Fixing broken operations increases flow simply because we frequently must stop to fix a broken operation or task. There should be no broken tasks within a healthcare production cell.

Eliminating unnecessary waits and non-value-added tasks and operations clearly increases flow.

Combining operations that are located near one another will frequently create a production cell automatically when we eliminate the walks and waits between operations. Sometimes, however, to create an efficient cell we must *colocate* operations that have been located in different areas, thereby eliminating transportation and motion waste.

Rearranging the order of operations can also promote flow when the current arrangement requires unnecessary backtracking to previous steps in the process.

And, of course, it always makes sense to *standardize and simplify* (see *Standard Work for Healthcare,* T. L. Jackson, editor, New York: Productivity Press, 2011) in order to reduce variation and to make defects, mistakes, and abnormal conditions obvious.

Take Five

Take 5 minutes to think about these questions and to write down your answers:

1. What do you think the takt time might be for a service family in which you are involved?
2. Are there any areas in your facility that already function as a clinical cell?

Example

Figure 5.5 shows an example of a nursing cell designed to serve patients in four contiguous rooms that have been assigned to a care team consisting of a registered nurse and a medical assistant. Commonly needed equipment and supplies are stored in the rooms at the point of use to eliminate unnecessary walking and transportation. The care team charts at bedside on tablets or a mobile computer.

An outpatient cell, designed to serve patients in two contiguous rooms assigned to a care team consisting of a physician and a medical assistant, is shown in Figure 5.6. Again, commonly used equipment and supplies are stored at point of use and clinicians and staff chart in the rooms. In addition, out-of-cycle work (pharmacy refill, lab result report, and other short-cycle work) is placed in the *heijunka* box so that those products can keep flowing also.

In Figure 5.7, we see how eliminating the waits (triangles) in the emergency room current-state map (Figure 4.11 in Chapter 4) results in an emergency

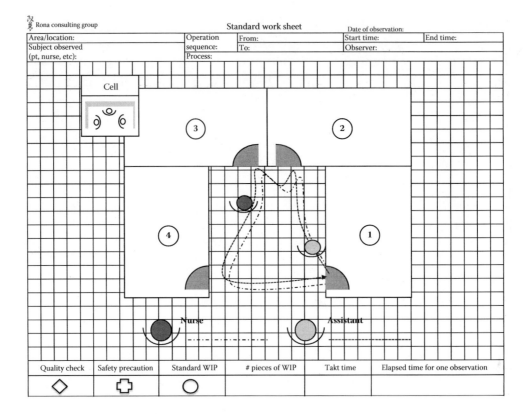

Figure 5.5 Nursing cell.

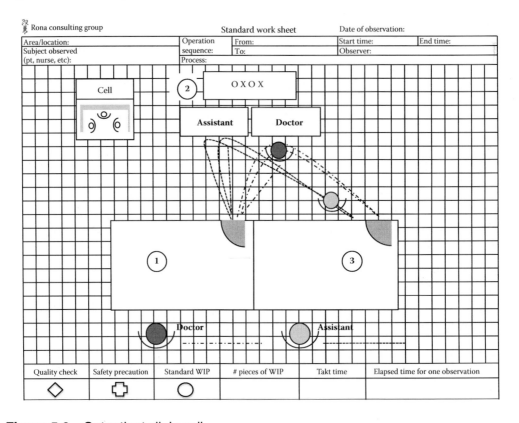

Figure 5.6 Outpatient clinic cell.

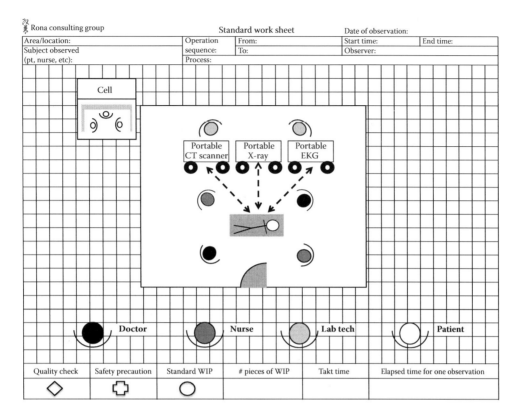

Figure 5.7 Emergency department high-acuity cell.

department cell designed to treat highly acute patients. The cell might be designed to exist within a single room, in which case we would expect to find portable x-ray and CT devices that eliminate the need to transport the patient around the hospital. If such services were available within the emergency department itself, the entire emergency department could be considered a production cell with respect to acute patients.

In the case of our ready-care value stream, the value stream mapping team has identified a couple of opportunities to create cells. The first cell the team proposes is a registration-assessment cell, where patients are registered by a registration clerk in the examination room and immediately assessed by an RN. The second cell proposed is an assess-treat cell, where patients are assessed by an MD and immediately treated by the MD or treatment nurse (Figure 5.8).

Background
INFO

Where Did All the People Go?

As stated in Chapter 1, value stream mapping was introduced to the world in 1998 with the publication of John Shook and Mike Rother's book, *Learning to See* (see Appendix). Subsequently, in the wake of the phenomenon called "Lean–Six Sigma," many hybrid mapping methods have been given the name "value stream map." This has created some confusion, particularly around the use of the cell icon.

Figure 5.8 Clinical cell in a ready-care value stream. Within the cell, the patient is simultaneously registered and assessed and does not wait between the two operations.

Some people, seeing this icon for the first time, wonder: Where did all the people go? The reason for the confusion is that they are more familiar with basic process mapping, which tends to represent visually the work of each and every staff member as a separate box in an operation or process.

The whole point to the cell icon, as employed in the original method, is to represent visually how operations in a process might be *combined and organized to produce according to takt time.* The additional detail necessary to set up and manage the resulting cell does not appear on the value stream map. Value stream maps typically focus at a higher level by mapping the flow across *multiple* cells. The detail required to create and manage a clinical cell is contained in the standard work documentation, as described in *Standard Work for Healthcare.* This documentation includes a standard work sheet, which defines the physical layout of the cell; a time observation form for each operator in the cell; a percent load chart, which describes how the operators work together; and other important documentation. (See Figure 5.9.)

5.3 SUMMARY

In Chapter 5 we introduced the first two principles of Lean healthcare production:

1. Produce services to takt time.
2. Eliminate unnecessary waits and create clinical cells.

Takt time is defined as the time available for service divided by the average demand for that period. It expresses the average rate at which patients must exit the value stream in order to prevent the need to make patients wait or

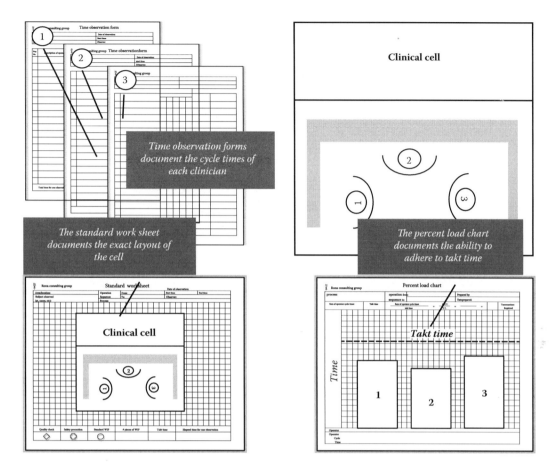

Figure 5.9 Where did all the people go? Time observations forms, standard work sheets, and percent load charts are normally sufficient to capture information about individual clinicians that previously appeared in process flow charts.

make clinicians work overtime. When all processes within the value stream are capable of meeting takt time, the production of healthcare services can be synchronized with actual demand throughout the day. Clinicians do not fall behind in their work, and patients do not wait.

The state of "not waiting" is defined as *flow*. Flow is achieved by eliminating unnecessary waits and delays (represented on the value stream map by the triangle "wait" icons) and by combining processes to form clinical cells. Within a cell, healthcare operations that are normally separated by different locations, levels of licensure, equipment, etc., are combined. Within a cell, clinicians work closely together as a team, and patients are transferred immediately from one clinical operation to the next. This is called "continuous flow" because it is uninterrupted by the seven non-value-added wastes.

5.4 REFLECTIONS

Now that you have completed this chapter, take 5 minutes to think about these questions and write down your answers:

- What did you learn from reading this chapter that stands out as being particularly useful or interesting to you in healthcare?
- How do you feel about the idea of "producing" healthcare services using industrial methods?
- Do you have any questions about the topics presented in this chapter? If so, what are they?
- Are there any special obstacles in your mind or the minds of your colleagues to applying the distinction between process and operation or the five key principles of Lean management in healthcare?
- What information do you still need to understand fully the ideas presented?
- How can you get this information?
- Whom do you need to involve in this process?

Chapter 6

Map the Future State— Phase II: Pull

6.1 INTRODUCTION

In Chapter 5 we explored the first two principles of a Lean healthcare production system:

1. Produce to takt time.
2. Flow the process.

In this chapter we will examine the remaining four principles (see Chapter 5, Figure 5.1):

3. If you cannot flow, pull.
4. Pull to the pacemaker.
5. Level the volume.
6. Level the mix.

Key Point

Before proceeding, however, it deserves to be repeated that *the ideal model for managing a Lean healthcare process is flow.* A process that flows is a process in which the patient never has to wait for care and care delivery is never interrupted by any of the seven wastes. In Chapter 5, we saw how ready-care operations could be connected to achieve flow by forming clinical cells. Of course, "flow the process" is easier said than done. It simply is not practical to combine *all* healthcare operations into a single, giant cell. After applying the first two principles of Lean healthcare production, we will still be faced with *multiple* cells or "islands of flow" that somehow must be integrated into a single stream of value for the benefit of the patient.

Key Point

While flow may be a useful ideal, it is often impractical for three reasons:

1. It may be physically impossible to combine two processes into a single cell because of distance, architecture, staffing, or other circumstances.
2. *Constraints* in the process can back up production, causing patients to wait for lengthy, often unpredictable amounts of

Definition

time. *A process constraint is any operation in a process that cannot meet takt time or is so critical to the process that any problem at that operation disrupts flow both upstream and downstream in the process.*

3. The sickest patients often need to violate the ideal of flow and step "out of line." For example, patients frequently wait in emergency department beds for admission to the hospital because the hospital discharge process is slow. Hospital beds are full of patients ready to go home; meanwhile, the paperwork is not ready or the attending physician cannot be found to sign it.

6.2 IF YOU CANNOT FLOW, PULL

P

Principle

When patients cannot be served one at a time because of their medical conditions or must wait because of a process constraint downstream, "pull" the patient to the downstream process, but only when that process is ready to produce the service required.

Definition

The general method of linking individual production cells into an integrated value stream is called *pull. Pull is a method for creating a system of production in which a downstream process—producing to takt time—signals to an upstream process that the downstream process is ready for the next patient.* Pull systems control both the production of healthcare services and the movement and wait times of patients between processes that cannot be combined into a production cell.

Definition

The signals employed by pull systems are called *kanban.* In Japanese, *kanban* means "signal card." *Kanban refers to any type of signal—physical or electrical—that is used by downstream processes to communicate readiness for production to upstream processes. (In materials management systems, kanban are also used to signal the need for more materials, medicines, and supplies.)* The use of kanban follows five rules, listed in Figure 6.1. In a system governed by these rules, the production of healthcare services is effectively synchronized throughout an entire value stream.

1. Downstream processes signal to upstream processes when they are ready for the next patient.
2. Upstream processes do not send patients to downstream processes until they receive a kanban or signal; they begin production on their own next patient *only once they have sent the last patient downstream.*
3. All processes produce and deliver only 100% defect-free services to their patients.
4. To synchronize production, it is leveled across all processes, preventing overproduction and waiting.
5. The kanban that govern the production of services for a patient tend to travel with the patient.

Figure 6.1 Rules of kanban.

This chapter explores two types of pull systems:

1. Pull with FIFO (first-in/first-out) lanes. With FIFO lanes, everyone has to "stay in line."
2. Pull with buffers. With buffers, production managers can vary the order and timing of production based upon emergent patient requirements.

Fortunately, healthcare organizations usually have good data that can tell us, on average, how many people will ask for help and how sick they will be. By looking at history, we can predict—often with astonishing precision—just how many patients will arrive (and in what order), how many will be able to "stay in line," and how many will need to "jump the queue" because of their medical condition. Meanwhile, although we may not have calculated the takt times for all our processes just yet and we may not always have the best information about *why* downstream processes (such as the discharge process) fail, we can study these phenomena by going to gemba and building a current-state map. With historical data and a current-state map in hand, we will be in a good position to plan for the inevitable. This is where pull systems come in.

Take Five

Take 5 minutes to think about these questions and to write down your answers:

1. When do we use "pull" systems to prioritize work?
2. What is a kanban and how is it used?

6.3 LINK SEPARATE PROCESSES WITH FIFO LANES

Key Point
When physical separation of processes prevents combining them into cells, the processes may be linked by controlling the time that patients wait between those operations. *The simplest way to create pull between two production cells or processes is to place strict limits on both the number and order of the patients between those cells or processes.* This can be achieved by using a concept known as a FIFO lane.

Definition

FIFO
FIFO means "first in/first out" and refers to well-regulated, short queues in which all inputs—in this case, patients—are processed in the same order in which they originally lined up. A FIFO lane is positioned after the completion of an upstream operation in which patients wait only a short, predetermined time before they are passed, one at a time, to a downstream process.

FIFO lanes stand in sharp contrast to the triangle icons introduced in Chapter 4. Triangle icons represent *unmanaged* queues; patients cannot predict the length of their waits and may not leave in an orderly way. (See Figure 6.2.) Obviously, patients in a FIFO lane must have their pain well managed and be of low acuity or, at least, in stable condition.

A FIFO lane is a potent control mechanism because it establishes either (1) a maximum number of patients who may be kept waiting in the lane or (2) a maximum time that any given patient may be asked to wait in the lane. (See Figure 6.3.) Ideally, when a FIFO lane fills up to its maximum number of patients (or, equivalently, at least one patient in the lane has been waiting the maximum time), the upstream process stops producing healthcare services. In other words, a full FIFO lane is a signal or kanban sent by the downstream process to the upstream process that no more patients

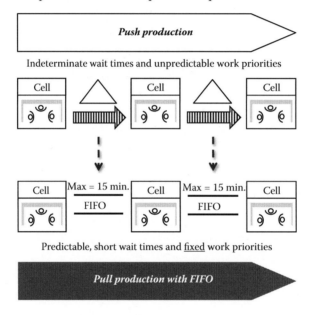

Figure 6.2   If you cannot flow, pull.

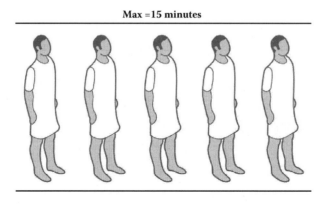

Figure 6.3   Stay in line, please. Within a FIFO lane, patients must stay in their original order.

are required at the moment. Only once the FIFO lane begins to empty is the upstream process authorized to produce more healthcare services and send patients downstream. One empty spot in a FIFO lane authorizes the upstream process to deliver service to one more patient. Two empty spots in a FIFO lane authorize the upstream process to deliver services to two more patients, and so on. In this manner, the upstream and downstream processes synchronize their production. No process gets ahead; no process falls behind. (See Figure 6.1, rule 2.)

As a practical matter, however, upstream processes do get ahead and downstream processes can fall behind. FIFO lanes that remain full or overfill signal management that either the upstream process is overproducing or the downstream process is not keeping up with takt time. This triggers corrective action by management to slow down the upstream process to takt time and/or help the downstream process speed up.

6.3.1 FIFO Lanes and Reaction Plans

What happens when a FIFO lane is full or when a patient has waited the maximum time allowed? If we do not react, we will be back in the world of "push," where patients arrive at the next operation in the process without regard to the readiness of clinicians to serve them. In manufacturing, we can simply turn off the production of inputs at the upstream process. This is impractical in healthcare, especially in an emergency department, where it would mean that we would simply stop admitting patients into the value stream.

Key Point

In healthcare, when a FIFO lane is full, a reaction plan must come into play that reallocates resources to flex our capacity upward a notch momentarily in order to reduce the number of patients waiting and the wait times experienced by patients in the FIFO lane. For this reason, when we implement a FIFO pull system, we must also put in place a monitoring system for FIFO lanes and ensure swift reaction to backup in the flow. In an emergency department, the charge nurse is an obvious choice to assume this new role. But effective management also requires careful planning and a willingness on the part of clinicians and staff members to help each other keep the flow moving. This means that when clinicians and staff have extra time during the ebb and flow of the day, they must switch from one operation to another for a short time. Obviously, this may in turn require cross-training and a very good system of real-time communication.

6.3.2 Where to Use FIFO Lanes

Key Point

In healthcare, FIFO lanes are useful in situations where patients do not need to "step out of line"—that is, situations in which patients are of low acuity and/ or are in stable condition. "Adherence FIFO" means that patients flow through the process in order; in other words, there are no queue jumpers. A good example of a situation in which FIFO can be applied in a healthcare value stream is cataract surgery. (See Figure 6.4.)

A wide variety of healthcare value streams can be organized to use clinical cells and FIFO lanes; these include imaging procedures, GI/endoscopy procedures, and all elective surgeries (e.g., orthopedic, ophthalmological, cosmetic, vascular, etc.). In each of these value streams, patients are normally of low acuity and in stable condition and have their pain well managed. Consequently, patients may move through the value stream without disrupting the first-in/first-out order set when the patients' procedures were initially scheduled. For an interesting example of a future-state map featuring pull systems based on FIFO in a vascular surgery value stream, see Baker and Taylor's *Making Hospitals Work* (Herefordshire, UK: Lean Enterprise Academy, 2009).

6.3.3 Is FIFO Consistent with Patient Safety?

To many clinicians, the idea of flow may at first seem counterintuitive or even counter to patient safety. Continuous flow permits no queue jumpers. That is, no patient is permitted to step out of line. In the *ideal* state of perfect FIFO, the same holds true. Patients would line up at the beginning of a process and then proceed in order through diagnosis, treatment, and discharge. Assuming that patients can be treated safely in such a manner, pull production with FIFO lanes will always be the most efficient way to run a value stream that cannot be consolidated into a single cell with continuous flow.

In healthcare, however, there are many queue jumpers. Patients "step out of line" because pain, acuity, or emergent conditions *demand* it. This is a matter of simple humanity as well as patient safety. Nevertheless, there are many instances when FIFO can be established and maintained in healthcare processes—particularly when patients are of low acuity, or at least in stable condition, and their pain has been managed effectively.

Principle

Furthermore, Lean thinking always posits the possibility of flow, even when it cannot be achieved as a practical matter. As a method, FIFO is not intended to "keep patients in line," but rather to encourage Lean thinkers to imagine new ways to eliminate the seven wastes introduced in Chapter 3, *thereby freeing capacity through more effective and efficient operations.* Every bit of capacity freed enables clinicians to deal more quickly and effectively with sick patients who need attention right now. FIFO, properly understood, helps improve patient safety as well as process efficiency.

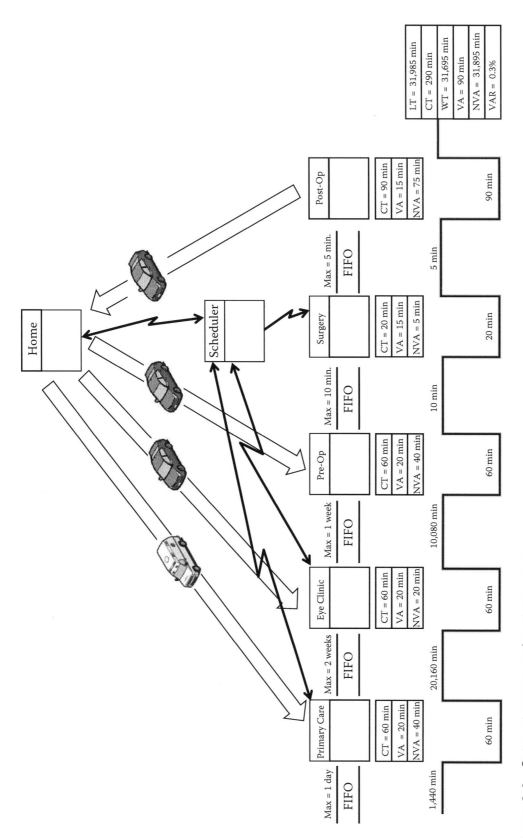

Figure 6.4 Cataract surgery value stream map.

6.4 PULL PRODUCTION WITH BUFFERS

We know that flow will be difficult to achieve when serving acutely ill patients in the emergency department because their medical conditions may require them to be processed in an order different from the order in which they arrive. The sickest patients often need to move to the head of the line, breaking the flow. The order in which very sick patients are served can also change from minute to minute, as their conditions worsen or improve. A patient presenting with chest pain automatically moves to the head of the line because he may be having a heart attack. (See Figure 6.5.) How can we manage this variability without disrupting the rest of the process?

In the case of FIFO lanes, we saw that—despite having to wait a bit from time to time—patients were always processed in a first-in/first-out order. To accommodate the predictable and frequently urgent need in healthcare to reshuffle patients (and to contain process variation associated with constraints such as the discharge process), pull systems employ *buffers*.

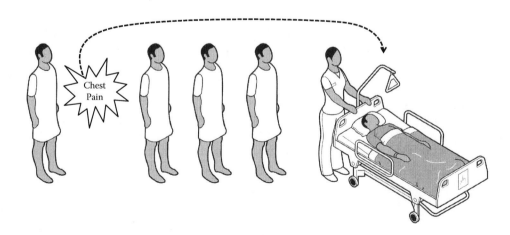

Figure 6.5 To the head of the line. Within a buffer, the order in which patients are processed may vary.

Definition
A buffer is a stock or supply of appropriately staffed and stocked exam rooms, beds, and other venues of care where patients are asked to wait a short, predetermined length of time under the appropriate level of care before moving to the next operation in the process. Buffers differ from FIFO lanes; patients in a buffer may or may not be served in the same order in which they arrived. In other words, the order in which patients in a buffer are served is not necessarily first in, first out. Thus, buffers offer flexibility in scheduling and rescheduling to accommodate sick patients who present symptoms that require them to go to the "head of the line." Also, buffers are typically larger than FIFO lanes, and therefore wait times within buffers typically are longer than wait times within FIFO lanes.

Background
INFO

n Beds Ahead

Loosely speaking, buffers of beds are nothing new in healthcare. Many nurse executives try to stay "a bed ahead" in the emergency room and in the hospital to promote the flow of patients through the system. But a buffer is *more* than a single bed. Actually, a buffer may be thought of as *n* beds (or other venues of care such as exam rooms) ahead, where *n* is determined based upon a statistical analysis of average demand. Generally speaking, the larger the buffer is, the less likely it is that we will fail to have a bed for the next patient. Without knowing the technicalities of pull systems, many healthcare organizations already use their observation units and universal care units to buffer throughput and achieve something like flow in the processes of their value streams. Of course, it would be impractical to ensure that we *always* have enough beds. But by carefully analyzing fluctuations (measured in terms of "standard deviations" or "sigmas") in average demand, we can establish buffer sizes that ensure a much higher service level than most healthcare organizations now provide.

Although buffers (and FIFO lanes as well) represent waiting—one of the seven deadly wastes—they also represent an organizational commitment to resolve the problem of waiting within a specified time frame. In particular, buffers protect the flow of patients who are able to "stay in line" by absorbing and managing variation in the process caused by sicker patients jumping the queue or by unreliable downstream processes. Correctly executed, buffers reduce or contain the normal, expected variation in our processes by making it *predictable*. (See Figure 6.6.)

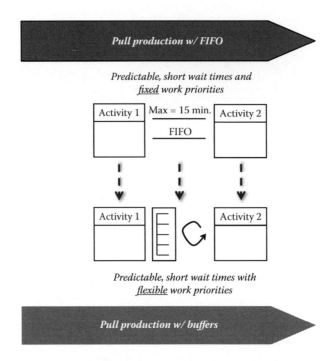

Figure 6.6 Pull production with buffers.

6.4.1 When to Use Buffers

In healthcare, buffers are often required in two situations:

1. They are often necessary whenever certain patients must move to the head of the line because of their medical condition. Moving to the head of the line breaks the flow by breaking the FIFO order, creating a kind of turbulence—like water tumbling over a rock.
2. They can be necessary whenever there are rate-limiting constraints in the healthcare process, such as the hospital discharge process.

Buffers are also required when two processes have different takt times.

6.4.2 Examples of Buffers

Example

In Figure 6.7, a buffer of appropriately staffed beds has been created to hold patients until emergency department cells are ready to provide services. Because of the buffer, patients in trauma may enter the value stream at any moment and move to the head of the line without endangering other sick patients who urgently need care. Another very practical implication of having such a buffer is that the emergency department will not need to divert patients to its competitors.

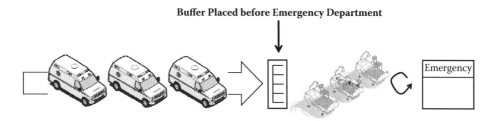

Figure 6.7 Buffer placed before emergency department. Which of the new arrivals will be served first?

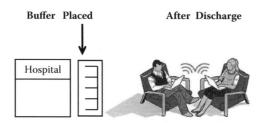

Figure 6.8 Buffer placed after discharge. This buffer protects flow in the hospital by freeing beds while patients ready to go home wait for transportation.

Let us assume that our patient has been admitted to the hospital and, after successful treatment and recovery, is ready to go home. In Figure 6.8, a buffer of appropriately staffed lounge chairs has been placed at the end of the process. As a result of adding this buffer, the hospital may now treat Sally (the sicker patient) while Sue (the patient to be discharged) waits comfortably and safely for her family to pick her up and take her home.

A good example of healthcare processes with different takt times would be the processes of the emergency department versus those of the hospital. (See Figure 6.9.) Recall that takt time equals net available time divided by average demand. As we know, emergency departments operate 24/7. Meanwhile, hospitals admit patients 24/7 but tend to discharge patients only during the day. So, the emergency department's net available time is greater than the hospital's net available time. In addition, the hospital admits patients from many different upstream processes, not just from its own attached emergency

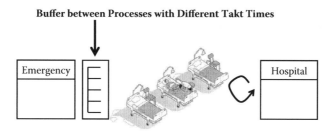

Figure 6.9 Buffer between processes with different takt times. This buffer protects flow in the emergency department and keeps patients safe while the hospital frees beds.

department. Thus, the hospital's average demand is different from the emergency department's average demand. It follows that there will be two different takt times: one for the emergency department and one for the hospital.

By adding a buffer of staffed beds between the emergency department and the hospital we accomplish two things. First, we free emergency department beds for new, often sicker patients. Second, we ensure the safety of patients being admitted while the hospital, patients' families, and other receiving agencies prepare to accept the patients who are ready to be discharged from the hospital.

Take Five

Take 5 minutes to think about these questions and to write down your answers:

1. What is a buffer?
2. Where might a buffer system be used in your operations?

6.4.3 Push Me, Pull You

Pull is the opposite of push production, in which patients move to the downstream process without regard to its readiness to accept them (as we saw in Chapter 4). Let us consider this, once again, because of the confusion that arises from the dual character of the patient.

As discussed in Chapter 3, the patient is both a customer of healthcare services and an input in the healthcare process. When thinking about push and pull, it is important to concentrate on the customer as input and to disregard (for a moment) the patient as customer. *All the information we require about the patient as customer is already taken into account in our calculation of takt time.* People sometimes say that in a Lean healthcare system, "patients pull themselves" through the process. This is a wrong conception of pull.

Principle

It is always the downstream process that "pulls" the patient as input, along with other inputs, such as medicines and supplies, to the place and moment of production. Moreover, the downstream operation pulls only when that operation is ready, not when the patient is ready. Ultimately, of course, the patient as customer stands at the very end of the value stream and "pulls" the patient as input through the process. But once the patient as customer signs a consent form, he becomes an input in the process of healthcare. Until he goes home, the downstream operations and processes of healthcare—not the patient—pull the patient as input through the process.

6.5 PULL TO THE PACEMAKER

Principle

Send the schedule of appointments to only one point in the process and then pull the patient from upstream operations to the pacemaker.

A Lean healthcare value stream sends the patient schedule to just one operation (called the *pacemaker*) in the value stream. Like the conductor of an orchestra (or the medical implant from which this Lean concept takes its name), the pacemaker sets the standard pace of healthcare service production (based on takt time) for all upstream processes so that everyone in the value stream knows what service to produce for the patient and when to produce it. Without a standard pace, the production of healthcare cannot be synchronized because our orchestra will have more than one conductor. And which conductor would we follow? The charge nurse? The emergency department physician? The hospitalist? The bed nurse?

The buffer icon, pull icon, and *heijunka* icons *always* appear together at the pacemaker process. (Heijunka is covered in more detail in Section 6.6.) This combination indicates that at the pacemaker operation or process, those responsible for scheduling patients can *vary* the pace and even the *order* of production. (See Figure 6.10.)

Example

In Figure 6.11, the hospital discharge process has been identified as the pacemaker for acutely ill patients entering the value stream through the emergency department. The pacemaker is positioned at the end of the healthcare value stream mainly because the condition of the patient often changes as a function of his disease process, the accuracy of the diagnosis, and responsiveness to treatment. In other words, there is a lot of uncertainty in the processes of healthcare that often cannot be worked out until the end. Thus, emergency department processes do not set the pace for the value stream.

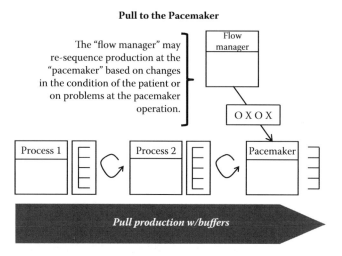

Figure 6.10 Pull to the pacemaker. The patient Is pulled by the next downstream process, but only when It is ready to serve the patient.

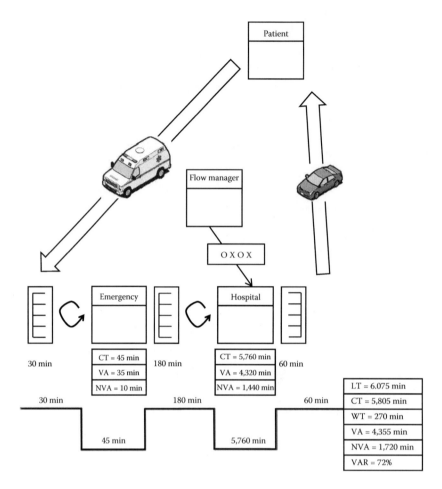

Figure 6.11 Acute care value stream.

In this example, continuous flow exists within the emergency department, which has been buffered twice: once to allow reprioritization of incoming cases and once again between the emergency department and hospital to ensure patient safety while patients wait for beds. It is ultimately the hospital's discharge process that determines how patients will complete their journey through the value stream. We will see precisely how this can be managed in Sections 6.6 and 6.7.

Background
INFO

Where Is the Pacemaker?

Before Toyota reinvented and decentralized production scheduling with pull systems, information about customer requirements was pooled in a central location, usually in a computer. Production instructions would be sent to every process in the value stream. It was hoped that computerized production scheduling would help synchronize production, but in practice it never worked very well. Because Lean production is *physically* synchronized *in real time* with pull systems, Toyota must send schedule information to only one process in the value stream—the pacemaker.

Technically speaking, the pacemaker will always be the last process in the value stream where the order of production routinely needs to be reshuffled or rearranged. Upstream of the pacemaker, patients cannot necessarily "stay in line" and the production of healthcare services cannot be FIFO. Upstream of the pacemaker, patients may "jump the queue," either because they randomly present symptoms of acute illness or because it helps clinicians to manage setup with respect to different diagnoses (without compromising patient safety, of course).

Downstream of the pacemaker, Lean production is all FIFO. Processes that have continuous flow or that are linked together by FIFO lanes do not require a downstream pacemaker. The order of production has already been set within the queue; the timing of production has been set by the cycle times of the respective processes and the maximum capacities of remaining FIFO lanes. Some people say that value streams in which processes are linked by FIFO lanes, such as elective surgery, are "unscheduled." This is not entirely correct. In a sense, the schedule itself is the pacemaker for a value stream integrated entirely by FIFO lanes and without buffers or heijunka.

Example

What other processes are pacemakers in the clinical setting? In the setting of psychiatric care, we find a universe that, in many respects, is parallel to acute care. Psychiatric patients in distress often enter the value stream through an emergency unit and, after being stabilized, spend time under intensive treatment in a psychiatric hospital unit before being discharged home. If patients are too ill to be discharged home, they may be transferred to long-term psychiatric care facilities, when space is available. So, if the patient's condition is sufficiently severe, the pacemaker may not be the discharge process (as was the case in Figure 6.11) but rather long-term care. (See Figure 6.12.) The availability of long-term facilities or—in extreme cases—locked facilities for psychiatric care is very limited, creating a process constraint far more intractable than discharges from the hospital.

6.6 LEVEL THE PRODUCTION VOLUME

Principle

At the pacemaker, schedule the production of healthcare services delivered to patients in small, regular increments of clinical work. This is called *leveling production volume*.

Leveling production by scheduling the production of healthcare services in regular increments (or bundles) of clinical work at the pacemaker operation

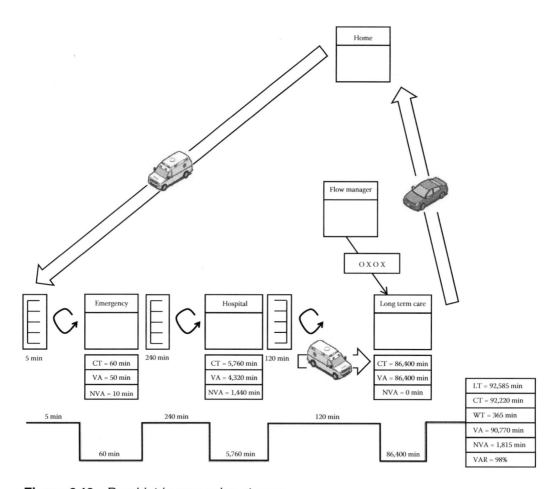

Figure 6.12 Psychiatric care value stream.

or process creates a regular, predictable rhythm throughout the value stream for patients and the clinicians who serve them. Once the pacemaker has been established as the single point of scheduling, *the entire value stream will take its cue from the pacemaker,* just as a patient's heart beats according to an electrical pulse, or an orchestra takes its cue from its conductor.

To understand the need for leveling the volume of healthcare service production, consider the perennial problem of managing discharges from the hospital. Assume that your hospital has 400 beds and that the average length of stay is 4 days. This means that you will discharge approximately 100 patients a day. Now assume that these discharges may take place anytime between the hours of 8:00 a.m. and 8:00 p.m. The time available for discharges is 12 hours or 720 minutes. The takt time is 720 minutes divided by 100 discharges, or 7.2 minutes. If you happened to be sitting in the medical center's parking lot, on average you would see one discharged patient exit the hospital every 7.2 minutes. From the patient's perspective, it would be wonderful if the system were capable of performing discharges at takt time. That way, anyone ready to leave could be discharged almost immediately without waiting for nurses to educate, doctors to round, labs to return, or transport to be available.

No management system in healthcare, however, is capable of keeping up such a pace. Discharges from the hospital are hostage to many realities. Nurses often do not begin the discharge process "upon admission" and delay many elements such as patient education until the last minute. Doctors frequently round on patients later in the day, instead of throughout the day. Labs are batched and doctors must wait to interpret results. Transport personnel are in short supply, and although they are not busy in the morning (when few discharges occur for the aforementioned reasons), in the afternoon—after doctors have made their rounds—suddenly there are many discharges and many patients who need to be transported to their waiting cars. The result is that many discharges occur late in the day and much more slowly than we would wish. Patients ready to go home must wait twice: once to be discharged and again to leave their hospital beds and go home. This is precisely the type of situation that leveling the volume is intended to prevent.

Background
INFO

"Bolus" as Evidence of Bogus Variation

A favorite phrase among clinicians is a "bolus of patients." According to the online Webster Dictionary, *bolus* means "1. A rounded mass, as: a) a large pill; b) a soft mass of chewed food." The term is used to refer to a mass of patients, suggesting the sudden arrival of a large group of uninvited guests. For clinicians, "bolus" defines the very real experience of *unanticipated* and hence *unmanaged* variation in the healthcare process. Indeed, the phenomenon of "push" explored in Chapter 4 explains why clinicians feel this way. In the clinical setting, push means precisely that patients arrive at the next operation before clinicians are ready to help them. Future-state mapping helps clinicians to rethink how patients move from operation to operation and, using historical data, to control process transitions and improve healthcare's readiness to serve. A "bolus of patients" is very often the consequence of not having thought through the healthcare process—or our own historical data—from an industrial, operations management perspective. In other words, the bolus is bogus variation in the process that is often (inadvertently) self-inflicted.

While it may be impossible to schedule discharges to occur one at a time according to takt time, let us consider a less demanding discharge schedule that avoids the problems associated with healthcare's default mode: massive batching of discharges at the end of the day. What if we could schedule discharges to occur at least four times a day, at 11:00 a.m., 2:00 p.m., 5:00 p.m., and 8:00 p.m.?

Definition

The schedule increment (in this case every 3 hours) is known as the "pitch," *which is also the name for the distance between airplane seats.* As anyone who travels by air knows, the greater the distance between airplane seats (that is, the greater the pitch) is, the greater is the comfort level in terms of leg room, privacy, angle to which your seat will recline, etc. Similarly, the greater the pitch in production scheduling is, the greater our management reaction time frame will be. The greater the pitch is, the less frequently we have to "go to gemba" to match the production of discharges to actual demand for discharges by making sure that nurses start discharge instruction upon admission and that doctors make rounds as frequently as needed—and on time.

Takt versus Pitch

We covered the concept of *takt time* in Chapter 5. Pitch introduces a new Lean measure of time and a new level of complexity. What is the difference between takt and pitch? In a word: *practicality.* Takt time is the average time (measured in minutes, in healthcare) in which patients must exit the process or value stream in order to satisfy market demand. Pitch is a longer, more practical time frame designed for the flow manager to stop and ask: Is this process producing according to takt time?

OXOX   The icon for level production is the "OXOX," or *heijunka,* icon. An example of a level production box is shown in Figure 6.13.

Definition   *When applied to hospital discharges, the level production or heijunka box is* *a device—very much like a mailbox—used to spread production of discharges* *evenly throughout the day.* The heijunka box in Figure 6.13 has been designed for a hospital organized on four floors. The floor numbers appear on the left side of the box, while the discharge times appear at the top. Each slot in the mailbox stands for discharges scheduled to take place at a particular time

	8:00–11:00	11:00–2:00	2:00–5:00	5:00–8:00
Floor 1	1	5	9	1 3
Floor 2	1 7	2 1	2 5	2 9
Floor 3	3 3	3 7	4 1	4 5
Floor 4 (maternity)	4 9	5 3	5 7	6 1

Figure 6.13 Hospital heijunka: level the volume.

74

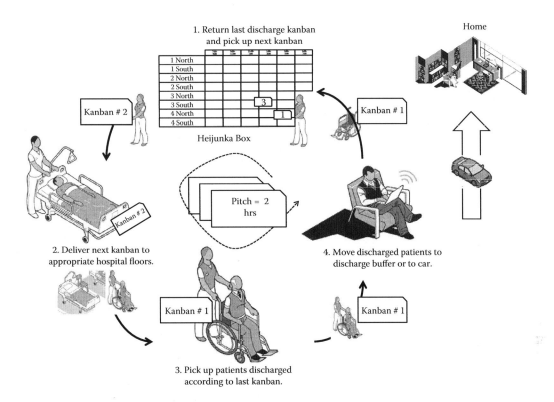

Figure 6.14 Example of paced hospital discharge.

from a particular floor. Discharge instructions for specific patients are hand-written or printed on kanban cards and placed in their respective slots.

Example

In Figure 6.14 we see how a pull system for discharges helps to level dis-charge volume and prevent the "train wreck" of discharges late in the day, with which we are all too familiar. In this system, the transport department plays a critical role. Instead of reacting to the normal flurry of transport requests late in the day, transport personnel have turned the tables on the entire system. *Transport* communicates to all four floors exactly when specific discharges are to occur and also transports patients to their cars or to special buffers or discharge hospitality centers* where they can wait for pickup. So radically different is the role that transport staff play in the new environment of Lean healthcare, we prefer to call them "discharge specialists."

The discharge pull system works this way:

1. The discharge specialist takes the kanban cards for patients scheduled to be discharged in the next "pitch" interval from the heijunka box. In

---

* Although the use of discharge lounges in hospitals has yielded mixed results to date, they might be improved by keeping the patient at the center of concern and communicating effectively to all staff. The potential benefit is that beds can become available sooner for sicker patients. For more information, see the paper "Discharge Lounge That Works: A Pathway for Implementation," by T. Hagerty, C. Clemente, and A. Sachdeva, MD (http://capitalmarketingservices.com/links/ Discharge_Lounge_PI-2.pdf).

other words, the discharge specialist visits the heijunka box once every 2 hours. Beforehand, hospital schedulers have evaluated their patients' readiness for discharge and the healthcare system's readiness to support the discharge process, and they have reshuffled the kanban accordingly.

2. Next, the transport specialist takes the newly prioritized kanban to the nursing floors, where the patients who are ready to be prepared for discharge lie in their beds, and delivers the kanban to the charge nurse.

3. As the discharge specialist leaves the floor, he or she transports patients discharged according to the *last* set of discharge kanban to a special discharge lounge (or directly to their cars, if their families are ready to drive the patients home).

4. In the discharge lounge, patients wait (under the appropriate level of care) until they are transported home. Meanwhile, the discharge specialist returns to the heijunka box to retrieve additional, newly prioritized discharge kanban to be distributed for the next pitch interval.

A New Role for Transport?

In today's hospital culture, transport personnel are nowhere near the top of the management pyramid. But in a Lean hospital, their role is radically transformed. Instead of responding to uncoordinated requests to transport patients while doctors and nurses wait impatiently, transport personnel in a Lean hospital drive the production of discharges (and other events) by delivering kanban, or production signals, that trigger paced discharges. Thus, the role of transport is virtually identical to that of materials managers—sometimes called "water spiders" because, in Lean manufacturing facilities, they flit effortlessly around the factory like the long-legged waterborne insects of summer. In manufacturing, materials management personnel carry production kanban to each unit to trigger production and remove finished goods to the final goods inventory warehouse to await shipment.

In a Lean hospital, transport personnel—which we have restyled as "discharge specialists"—carry production kanban to each area of the hospital to trigger discharges and remove discharged patients to their cars or to the discharge lounge to await pickup. Materials management personnel (and, by extension, our discharge specialists) are the nervous system of a Lean production system because, without the delivery of production kanban, no goods (and, in the hospital setting, no discharges) would be produced. So vital is this role that even the president of Toyota himself is not permitted to interrupt a "water spider" as he navigates his route through one of Toyota's factories.

Take Five

Take 5 minutes to think about these questions and to write down your answers:

1. What do we call the operation in a value stream to which the schedule is sent?
2. What do we mean by leveling production volume in a health-care setting?
3. Are there operations in your area where you experience a "bolus of patients"? Can you think of one or two ideas that might improve this unmanaged variation?

6.7 LEVEL THE CASE MIX

Principle

At the pacemaker, distribute production of different healthcare services (diagnoses) as evenly as possible to improve the synchronization of production throughout the value stream.

Of course, there are discharges, and then there are *discharges*. We must pay attention not only to the *volume* of discharges but also to the case *mix*. It is quite possible to level the volume of discharges and still end up with problems if we do not pay attention to the case mix. For example, we might level the volume on average for the hospital as a whole without discharging enough male patients. This would result, of course, in a shortage of male beds, which could impede the flow of male patients throughout the system. The emergency department might even be forced to go on divert, as beds for males filled up awaiting admission to the hospital. To ensure that both male and female patients flow through the system, we must spread throughout the day not only the total volume of patients but also the mix of male and female patients. Fortunately, the discharge specialist, armed with an appropriately designed heijunka box, is well positioned to manage both volume and mix.

Example

Let us now assume that our hospital is a part of an integrated medical center where we see males and females. Each case type is accommodated on each floor (or portion thereof) in the hospital, except floor 4, which is a perinatal unit (what we used to call a "maternity ward") specializing in females only. In Figure 6.15, the heijunka box has been redesigned to manage the mix of males and females as well as the total volume of discharges. Special discharge kanban have been created for each case type. The heijunka box and the new discharge kanban will be used to manage both the volume and the mix of discharges in the hospital.

The system works exactly as shown previously in Figure 6.14, except now, when the discharge specialist picks up a set of kanban for each pitch interval

	8:00–11:00	11:00–2:00	2:00–5:00	5:00–8:00
Floor 1	1	5	9	1 3
Floor 2	1 7	2 1	2 5	2 9
Floor 3	3 3	3 7	4 1	4 5
Floor 4 (maternity)	4 9	5 3	5 7	6 1

Figure 6.15   Hospital heijunka: level the case mix.

at the heijunka box, each kanban will contain instructions for discharging a patient of a particular case type. If the flow manager for the hospital is careful to distribute the volume and mix of male and female discharges across the entire day, there should be a steady stream of male and female patients throughout the day. Obviously, the mix of cases could be much more complex, accommodating patients with different medical conditions as well as patients of different sex. Pull systems are completely flexible and can accommodate different diagnoses as well as different genders.

In clinical value streams, heijunka can be used to level the volume and mix of more than just patients. In Figure 6.16 we see a heijunka box used in an outpatient clinic to level the volume and mix of patients and *paperwork*. In this case, while patients may flow through the clinic in more or less a first-in/first-out fashion, we must accommodate the clinicians' responsibility for a vast amount of "noncyclical work" associated with their patient population (not necessarily for the patient they happen to be with at the moment). This work includes evaluating results from laboratory tests, returning phone messages, responding to prescription refill requests, filling out insurance papers, charting, and so forth. In the outpatient clinical setting, such work is voluminous (more so in hospitals with large indigent or undocumented patient populations) and can back up quickly, often resulting in the need for clinicians to work many hours after their clinics close. By means of the pull system pictured in Figure 6.16, such noncyclical work is prioritized by the flow manager and released in small increments at the heijunka box.

Example

At Virginia Mason Medical Center in Seattle, Washington, such heijunka boxes were positioned at "flow stations" between contiguous exam rooms. Between each patient encounter, clinicians stopped at their flow stations, executed a few pieces of the prioritized work, and moved on to see their next patient, who had already been registered and roomed. As a result of implementing flow stations in all outpatient clinics, clinicians who once complained of working late were able to join their families at the dinner table—and the

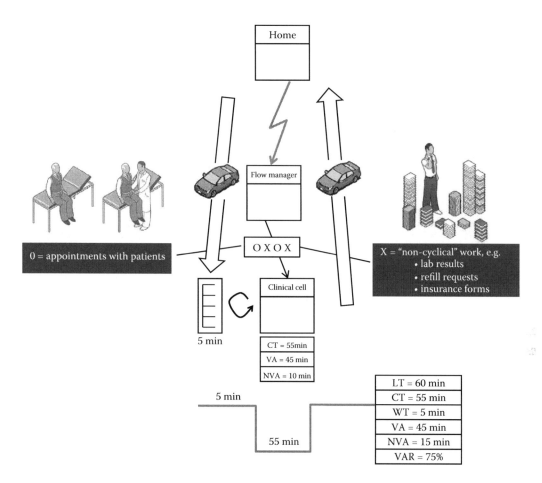

Figure 6.16 Pull production in an outpatient setting.

clinics, which once lost money, became profitable. Such is the power of Lean thinking, clinical production cells, and pull systems.

6.8 SUMMARY

If you cannot *flow* by reorganizing operations and processes into the production cells we introduced in this chapter, then you must *pull* by one of two methods that regulate the amount of time that patients are asked to wait between separate processes in your value stream. Pull production is the Lean alternative to push production. In a push environment, patients wait between processes, but do not know how long they may wait or in what order clinicians will process them. Patients are "pushed" through the value stream from process to process without regard to clinicians' readiness to receive them, and consequently patients wait.

The first way to avoid "push" is to connect individual processes or cells by means of appropriately staffed and monitored *FIFO lanes*. Within a FIFO (first-in/first-out) lane, patients wait a short, predetermined length of time and exit the lane in the same order in which they entered. In effect, the work priorities of clinicians in the process directly downstream of a FIFO lane are fixed because there is no opportunity to reshuffle the order of patients according to their respective conditions or diagnoses. Thus, FIFO lanes are useful in situations where patients are of low acuity or are in stable condition and pain is under control.

The second way to avoid "push" is to connect individual processes or cells by means of appropriately staffed and monitored *buffers*. Within a buffer, patients wait a short, predetermined length of time, but may exit the buffer in a different order in which they entered. In effect, the work priorities of the process directly downstream of a buffer remain flexible because patients may be reshuffled depending upon their diagnosis or upon unexpected changes in their respective conditions. Thus, buffers are useful in situations where patients are of high acuity or otherwise are not in stable condition.

Within a value stream that contains FIFO lanes but no buffers, the schedule sets the pace of production. Where buffers are used, it is necessary to identify a pacemaker process to which the initial schedule may be sent. Normally, the pacemaker process is near the end of the value stream, which permits upstream processes to adjust their work priorities as patients' conditions evolve in response to treatment. To facilitate the synchronization of all processes in the value stream, patients are treated at the pacemaker in relatively small increments or "batches." This is called *heijunka*, or leveling, which can be applied to both the volume of patients and the case mix.

6.9 REFLECTIONS

Now that you have completed this chapter, take 5 minutes to think about these questions and write down your answers:

- What did you learn from reading this chapter that stands out as being particularly useful or interesting to you in healthcare?
- How do you feel about the idea of "leveling" the volume and mix of healthcare production?
- Do you have any questions about the topics presented in this chapter? If so, what are they?
- Are there any special obstacles in your mind or the minds of your colleagues to applying the concepts of FIFO lanes or buffers in healthcare?
- What information do you still need to understand fully the ideas presented?
- How can you get this information?
- Whom do you need to involve in this process?

Chapter 7

Implement the Future State

7.1 FOCUS

One of the major pitfalls of beginning improvement work in any industry is to take a shotgun approach and try to improve everything at once. Because there is so much work to be done (and all of it is worthwhile), it is easy to lose focus. It has been more than a decade since the Institute of Medicine's landmark book, *To Err Is Human,* revealed that as many as 98,000 patients die in hospitals each year as the result of avoidable medical errors.* The healthcare industry has worked diligently to improve; however, while there certainly have been many "points of light" since then, overall, nothing much has changed. In fact, things have gotten worse. It is time for a very different approach.

By constructing a large-scale future-state map, you have already taken an important step toward protecting yourself from strategic confusion and deadlock. Your future-state map will help you keep your "eyes on the prize" of patient safety and quality.

7.2 LOOP THE "LOOPS"

Definition

To stay focused during implementation, break the value stream down into *value stream loops,* which will be connected to produce a family of related healthcare services. *A value stream loop (or "loop," for short) is a discrete subsystem of patient services.* Typically, a loop consists of several processes that can be simplified and standardized, perhaps even combined and colocated to create a single production cell.

Key Point

Normally, each loop will be associated with its own variation-absorbing FIFO (first-in/first-out) lane or buffer positioned at the end of the loop. Each loop begins with the patient entering a specific process and ends with the patient waiting—in a FIFO lane or buffer—to enter the next process in the value stream. Constructing an inte-

---

* Institute of Medicine, L. T. Kohn, J. M. Corrigan, and M. S. Donaldson, eds. *To Err Is Human: Building a Safer Health System* (Washington, DC: National Academy Press, 2000). Cf. 2009 National Healthcare Quality Report (Rockville, MD: US Department of Health and Human Services Agency for Healthcare Research and Quality, 2010).

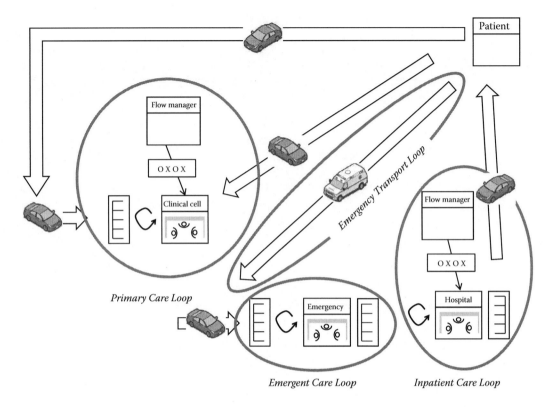

Figure 7.1 Value stream implementation loops.

grated clinical value stream is something like snapping construction blocks together, with FIFO lanes and buffers acting as connectors.

Example

Figure 7.1 shows a consolidated value stream map for the medical center we have investigated throughout this book. In this value stream there are at least four loops, each with its own takt time:

1. The inpatient care (hospital) or "pacemaker" loop
2. The emergent care loop
3. The primary care loop
4. The emergency transportation loop

The circles drawn on the map help you see where you need to concentrate your improvement efforts. During implementation, each loop becomes a focal point for improvement activity.*

The crux of the value stream is the pacemaker loop, which establishes the flow of information between patients and the pacemaker process. The design and management of the pacemaker loop will affect the design and management of all the other loops in the system. Because the pacemaker loop is

---

* The four loops in Figure 7.1 are illustrative of the planning process. Additional loops are beyond the scope of this short book. One obvious omission, made for the sake of simplicity, is the surgery loop. In addition, we might treat ancillary and nonclinical value streams as separate loops.

normally found toward the end of the value stream, it provides the basic rhythm of production with which the independent rhythms of all other processes must be synchronized.

There is a natural correspondence between implementation loops and traditional healthcare service lines. Moreover, loops often can be associated with the major clinical, ancillary, and nonclinical processes we saw in Chapter 3, Figure 3.1. From time to time, loops may correspond to a particular diagnosis, such as congestive heart failure. Of course, the focus of this book has been on clinical processes and value streams, but inevitably you will need to map your feeder lines—the ancillary and nonclinical processes—as well, in order to construct value streams that span your entire healthcare enterprise.

7.3 HOSHIN KANRI, A3-TS, AND PDCA

Clearly, the implementation of Lean healthcare production in multiple loops is a big job. In fact, it will be the biggest job of your career. Such a job calls for an industrial-strength approach to project management. Toyota uses an approach called *hoshin kanri.*

Definition

The Japanese term "hoshin" means compass; the term "kanri" means management. Hoshin kanri is translated as "strategy management" or "policy deployment." Hoshin kanri ("hoshin" for short) resolves large-scale projects into multiple, smaller projects, each with its own project manager, or "executive sponsor." Each project is documented by means of a project plan called an A3, or A3-T team charter; the "A3" stands for the European paper size (29.7 × 42 centimeters—roughly the same size as 11 × 17 inch tabloid paper) on which the plans are printed. (See Figure 7.2.)

An A3-T is more than a project plan. It represents a complete cycle of organizational learning. Within Lean healthcare organizations, organizational learning is governed by the Deming cycle of PDCA (plan, do, check, and act),

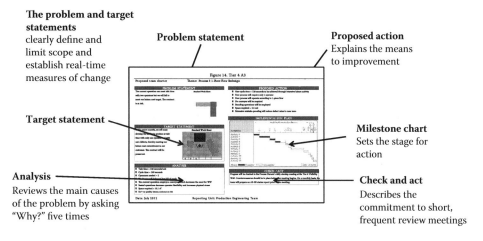

The problem and target statements clearly define and limit scope and establish real-time measures of change

Problem statement

Proposed action Explains the means to improvement

Target statement

Milestone chart Sets the stage for action

Analysis Reviews the main causes of the problem by asking "Why?" five times

Check and act Describes the commitment to short, frequent review meetings

Figure 7.2 Anatomy of an A3-T.

Plan	Walk the value stream and develop an improvement proposal by drafting an A3-T.
Do	Test the hypothesis through small trials of change in the context of 5-day kaizen workshops.
Check	Check results.
Act	Document successfully tested standards with new standard work instruction sheets.

Figure 7.3   PDCA for implementing the future state.

a concise version of the scientific method. (See Figure 7.3.) For more information about hoshin kanri, see *Hoshin Kanri for the Lean Enterprise: Building Capability and Managing Profit* (T. L. Jackson, Portland, OR: Productivity Press, 2006).

7.3.1 Plan: Write an A3-T for Each Loop

In the "plan" phase of hoshin, we walk the value stream and record our observations in the form of a current-state value stream map. Based upon our observations, we analyze the causes of long lead times and poor quality. This provides the basis for brainstorming improvements using the F-E-C-R-S method explained in Chapter 6 and for proposing effective process improvements in the form of a future-state value stream map. All of this is documented on the A3-T, together with a detailed milestone chart that records the *whos*, *whats*, and *whens* of implementation. In Figures 7.4, 7.5, and 7.6, we see examples of A3-Ts developed from the value stream mapping experiences for cataract surgery, emergency care, and psychiatric care.

7.3.2 Do: Conduct Kaizen Workshops

Typically, the improvements required to realize the future state are carried out through a series of 5-day kaizen workshops, which are recorded under the "implementation plan" section of the A3-T. See Figure 7.7 for a typical kaizen workshop agenda. For detailed information about how to organize and conduct a 5-day kaizen workshop, see *Kaizen Workshops for Lean Healthcare* (T. L. Jackson, editor, New York: Productivity Press, 2012).

In most cases, the initial workshops will focus on reorganizing the workplace, establishing standard work for all operations in your process, and consolidating disparate or uncoordinated operations into healthcare service production cells. As operations are standardized, fire-fighting stops and clinicians and support staff can begin to think about preventing process delays and defects. Standardization creates a context for something new: *measurement*. Without standards and adherence to standards, it is impossible to determine what is going on. Measuring something requires us to determine quantitative deviations from a standard. In the case of Lean healthcare operations, the standards

TEAM CHARTER | **Date:** 1-Nov-12 | **Reporting Unit:** CATARACT SURGERY | **Theme:** SURGERY WHEN YOU NEED IT

PROBLEM STATEMENT

Over the past 5 years, the lead time for cataract surgery has increased from 2 months to 12 months, while a large backlog of cases has continued to grow. Over the same time period, the number of surgery patients arriving in pre-op on the day of surgery without necessary lab work or H&Ps has risen from 10% to 25%.

Chart: CATARACT LOS (MOS), 2008–2012
Chart: NO LABS/H&P (%), 2008–2012

TARGET STATEMENT

By December 31, 2015, we will reduce the lead time for cataract surgery by over 90% to 31,985 minutes (from request for appointment to discharge from post-op). We will also reduce the number of surgery preparation defects (missing labs and H&Ps) to zero.

Chart: CATARACT LOS (MIN), 2012–2015
Chart: NO LABS H&P (%), 2012–2015

ANALYSIS

The current scheduling practice in eye clinics relies upon a scheduler to complete all paperwork after the patient has seen the physician. Most often, the scheduler must "follow up" to make appointments for H&P exams, labs and surgery *after the patient has left the clinic.* Neither the doctor, the nurse nor the patient see it as their job to participate in the scheduling process. This leads to an extremely time-consuming and frustrating "rabbit chase," with the scheduler trying to piece together what happened in the clinic, on the one hand, and trying to make contact with the patient, on the other hand. Ironically, despite herculean efforts to obtain correct information, schedulers are frequently blamed for "scheduling errors" that clearly are the result of a poorly designed process.

PROPOSED ACTIONS

We will implement a lean value stream by gearing the production of cataract surgery services to takt time. In a series of 5-day kaizen workshops (see below), we will smooth patient flow in primary care, the eye clinic, pre-op, surgery and post-op by eliminating patient waits and creating a detailed plan to work off the backlog of cataract cases.

IMPLEMENTATION PLAN

ACTION ITEM	RESPONSIBILITY	DUE DATE
Kaizen 1: 4-3-2-1 planning process	kaizen promotion office	Jan-13
Kaizen 1: 5-day workshop	workshop leader	Feb-13
Kaizen 1: 30-day kaizen action bulletin execution	process owner	Mar-13
Kaizen 1: 30-60-90 day validation process	kaizen promotion office	Aug-13
Kaizen 2: 4-3-2-1 planning process	kaizen promotion office	Mar-13
Kaizen 2: 5-day workshop	workshop leader	Apr-13
Kaizen 2: 30-day kaizen action bulletin execution	process owner	May-13
Kaizen 2: 30-60-90 day validation process	kaizen promotion office	Oct-13
Kaizen 3: 4-3-2-1 planning process	kaizen promotion office	May-13
Kaizen 3: 5-day workshop	workshop leader	Jun-13
Kaizen 3: 30-day kaizen action bulletin execution	process owner	Jul-13
Kaizen 3: 30-60-90 day validation process	kaizen promotion office	Dec-13
Kaizen 4: 4-3-2-1 planning process	kaizen promotion office	Jul-13
Kaizen 4: 5-day workshop	workshop leader	Aug-13
Kaizen 4: 30-day kaizen action bulletin execution	process owner	Sep-13
Kaizen 4: 30-60-90 day validation process	kaizen promotion office	Feb-14
Kaizen 5: 4-3-2-1 planning process	kaizen promotion office	Sep-13
Kaizen 5: 5-day workshop	workshop leader	Oct-13
Kaizen 5: 30-day kaizen action bulletin execution	process owner	Nov-13
Kaizen 5: 30-60-90 day validation process	kaizen promotion office	Apr-14
Kaizen 6: 4-3-2-1 planning process	kaizen promotion office	Nov-13
Kaizen 6: 5-day workshop	workshop leader	Dec-13
Kaizen 6: 30-day kaizen action bulletin execution	process owner	Jan-14
Kaizen 6: 30-60-90 day validation process	kaizen promotion office	Jun-14

CHECK AND ACT

We will monitor implementation of kaizen improvements through daily audits of standard work and weekly stand-up executive review meetings. We will maintain 5S at level 3 and develop a visual workplace to surface defects in real time. The kaizen promotion office will re-measure target completion and compile reports at 30, 60 and 90 days.

Figure 7.4 A3-T example 1: Cataract surgery process improvement. (From J. Michael Rona and Associates, LLC, doing business as Rona Consulting Group, copyright 2008–2013. http://www.ronaconsulting.com. All rights reserved. Reprinted with permission.)

TEAM CHARTER	Date: 1-Dec-12	Reporting Unit: ACUTE CARE	Theme: TIME FOR BED

PROBLEM STATEMENT

Over the past 5 years, the length of stay (LOS) in the ED has risen from 2 to 8 hours, while the LOS in the hospital has risen to 6 days. Meanwhile, patients in the ED sometimes wait more than 8 hours for admission to the hospital.

ED LOS (HRS) — chart (2008–2012)

HOSPITAL LOS (DAYS) — chart (2008–2012)

TARGET STATEMENT

By December 31, 2015, we will reduce LOS in the ED to 45 minutes and LOS in the hospital to 5,760 minutes (4 days). Meanwhile, patients will not wait more than 5 minutes to be seen in the ED. Patients will not wait more than 180 minutes to be admitted to the hospital floor from the ED.

ED LOS (HRS) — chart (2012–2015)

HOSPITAL LOS (DAYS) — chart (2012–2015)

ANALYSIS

In the ED, patients wait for admission to the hospital for a variety of reasons. Mainly, beds are not available in the hospital because the discharge process is constrained by nonstandard rounding processes and schedules employed by attending physicians. In addition, attending physicians act as gatekeepers to the hospital and are not always prompt in responding to requests from ED physicians who seek admission for their acute patients. Nursing practices in the hospital contribute to the problem in two ways. First, the discharge process is not begun upon admission, resulting in delays once discharge orders are written at the end of the patient stay. Second, nurses resist removing fragile patients from needed beds because friends and relatives are frequently late to transport patients to their homes.

PROPOSED ACTIONS

We will implement a lean acute care value stream by gearing the production of healthcare services to takt time. In a series of 5-day kaizen workshops (see below), we will smooth patient flow in the ED and in the hospital by eliminating unnecessary patient waits and installing a system of appropriately staffed buffers to absorb normal variation in demand.

IMPLEMENTATION PLAN

ACTION ITEM	RESPONSIBILITY	DUE DATE
Kaizen 1: 4-3-2-1 planning process	kaizen promotion office	Jan-13
Kaizen 1: 5-day workshop	workshop leader	Feb-13
Kaizen 1: 30-day kaizen action bulletin execution	process owner	Mar-13
Kaizen 1: 30-60-90 day validation process	kaizen promotion office	Aug-13
Kaizen 2: 4-3-2-1 planning process	kaizen promotion office	Mar-13
Kaizen 2: 5-day workshop	workshop leader	Apr-13
Kaizen 2: 30-day kaizen action bulletin execution	process owner	May-13
Kaizen 2: 30-60-90 day validation process	kaizen promotion office	Oct-13
Kaizen 3: 4-3-2-1 planning process	kaizen promotion office	May-13
Kaizen 3: 5-day workshop	workshop leader	Jun-13
Kaizen 3: 30-day kaizen action bulletin execution	process owner	Jul-13
Kaizen 3: 30-60-90 day validation process	kaizen promotion office	Dec-13
Kaizen 4: 4-3-2-1 planning process	kaizen promotion office	Jul-13
Kaizen 4: 5-day workshop	workshop leader	Aug-13
Kaizen 4: 30-day kaizen action bulletin execution	process owner	Sep-13
Kaizen 5: 4-3-2-1 planning process	kaizen promotion office	Feb-13
Kaizen 5: 5-day workshop	workshop leader	Sep-13
Kaizen 5: 30-day kaizen action bulletin execution	process owner	Oct-13
Kaizen 5: 30-60-90 day validation process	kaizen promotion office	Nov-13
Kaizen 6: 4-3-2-1 planning process	kaizen promotion office	Apr-13
Kaizen 6: 5-day workshop	workshop leader	Nov-13
Kaizen 6: 30-day kaizen action bulletin execution	process owner	Dec-13
Kaizen 6: 30-60-90 day validation process	kaizen promotion office	Jan-13
		Jun-13

CHECK AND ACT

We will monitor implementation of kaizen improvements through daily audits of standard work and weekly stand-up executive review meetings. We will maintain 5S at level 3 and develop a visual workplace to surface defects in real time. The kaizen promotion office will re-measure target completion and compile reports at 30, 60 and 90 days.

Figure 7.5 Example 2: Time for bed. (From J. Michael Rona and Associates, LLC, doing business as Rona Consulting Group, copyright 2008–2013. http://www.ronaconsulting.com. All rights reserved. Reprinted with permission.)

TEAM CHARTER	Date: 4-Jan-13	Reporting Unit: PSYCHIATRY	Theme: THERE'S A PLACE FOR YOU

PROBLEM STATEMENT

Over the past 5 years, the lead time of a psychiatric patient's experience from presentation in the ED to discharge from our inpatient psychiatric unit has grown from 5 to 20 days. During the same period, the number of non-acute administrative days not reimbursed by payers has risen from 25% to 60% of the total length of the inpatient stay.

Charts: ACUTE LEAD TIME (DAYS); NON-ACUTE DAYS (%) — 2008–2012

TARGET STATEMENT

By December 31, 2015, we will reduce the lead time from presentation in the ED to discharge from the inpatient psych unit by nearly 50% to 14,705 minutes (10.2 days). We will also reduce the number of non-acute administrative days to 30% of the total length of the inpatient stay.

Charts: ACUTE LEAD TIME (MIN); NON-ACUTE DAYS (%) — 2012–2015

ANALYSIS

The psychiatric value stream is responsible for a population of complex patients for whom reimbursement is not always available. Many days considered to be "non-acute" (and therefore non-reimbursable) by payers are clinically necessary for patient recovery. Many if not most non-acute patients require further care in specialized settings, but these are not well funded and therefore in very short supply. Intermediate and long-term psychiatric care facilities that might accept patients after discharge from the psych inpatient unit sometimes disagree about the clinical status of patients and also differ in their admitting criteria. This naturally leads to extended lengths of stay in the acute, inpatient setting and long waits for placement to more appropriate venues of care.

PROPOSED ACTIONS

We will implement a lean value stream by gearing production of services to takt time. In a series of 5-day kaizen workshops (see below), we will smooth patient flow in the psych ED and hospital by eliminating patient waits. We will also work closely with long-term care facilities to speed placement of non-acute patients who need further care.

IMPLEMENTATION PLAN

ACTION ITEM	RESPONSIBILITY	DUE DATE
Kaizen 1: 4-3-2-1 planning process	kaizen promotion office	Jan-13
Kaizen 1: 5-day workshop	workshop leader	Feb-13
Kaizen 1: 30-day kaizen action bulletin execution	process owner	Mar-13
Kaizen 1: 30-60-90 day validation process	kaizen promotion office	Aug-13
Kaizen 2: 4-3-2-1 planning process	kaizen promotion office	Mar-13
Kaizen 2: 5-day workshop	workshop leader	Apr-13
Kaizen 2: 30-day kaizen action bulletin execution	process owner	May-13
Kaizen 2: 30-60-90 day validation process	kaizen promotion office	Oct-13
Kaizen 3: 4-3-2-1 planning process	kaizen promotion office	May-13
Kaizen 3: 5-day workshop	workshop leader	Jun-13
Kaizen 3: 30-day kaizen action bulletin execution	process owner	Jul-13
Kaizen 3: 30-60-90 day validation process	kaizen promotion office	Dec-13
Kaizen 4: 4-3-2-1 planning process	kaizen promotion office	Jul-13
Kaizen 4: 5-day workshop	workshop leader	Aug-13
Kaizen 4: 30-day kaizen action bulletin execution	process owner	Sep-13
Kaizen 4: 30-60-90 day validation process	kaizen promotion office	Feb-13
Kaizen 5: 4-3-2-1 planning process	kaizen promotion office	Sep-13
Kaizen 5: 5-day workshop	workshop leader	Oct-13
Kaizen 5: 30-day kaizen action bulletin execution	process owner	Nov-13
Kaizen 5: 30-60-90 day validation process	kaizen promotion office	Apr-13
Kaizen 6: 4-3-2-1 planning process	kaizen promotion office	Nov-13
Kaizen 6: 5-day workshop	workshop leader	Dec-13
Kaizen 6: 30-day kaizen action bulletin execution	process owner	Jan-13
Kaizen 6: 30-60-90 day validation process	kaizen promotion office	Jun-13

CHECK AND ACT

We will monitor implementation of kaizen improvements through daily audits of standard work and weekly stand-up executive review meetings. We will maintain 5S at level 3 and develop a visual work-place to surface defects in real time. The kaizen promotion office will re-measure target completion and compile reports at 30, 60 and 90 days.

Figure 7.6 A3-T example 3: Psychiatric care process improvement. (From J. Michael Rona and Associates, LLC, doing business as Rona Consulting Group, copyright 2008–2013. http://www.ronaconsulting.com. All rights reserved. Reprinted with permission.)

Workshop schedule		
Mon.	11:00 a.m.	Train participants in Lean healthcare concepts and methods.
	1:30 p.m.	Review value stream map, A3, and targets for the workshop.
	2:30 p.m.	Go to gemba to observe and document additional process wastes.
	4:30 p.m.	Review progress and scope with workshop sponsor and process owner.
	5:00 p.m.	First day ends—focal points of improvement activity are well understood.
Tues.	8:00 a.m.	Prioritize improvement ideas and form improvement subteams.
	9:30 a.m.	Go to gemba: Observe the process; conduct small tests of change.
	4:30 p.m.	Review progress and scope with workshop sponsor and process owner.
	5:00 p.m.	Second day ends—process documentation is complete; more tests of change are planned.
Wed.	8:00 a.m.	Return to gemba to continue observations and tests of change.
	4:30 p.m.	Review progress and scope with workshop sponsor and process owner.
	5:00 p.m.	Third day ends—most tests of change completed.
Thurs.	7:00 a.m.	Conduct additional tests of change as required.
	8:00 a.m.	Draft new standard work instructions and plan in-service training.
	2:30 p.m.	Complete new process documentation and final presentation.
	3:30 p.m.	Practice presentation.
	5:00 p.m.	Fourth day ends—process documentation and presentation are complete.
Fri.	8:00 a.m.	Rehearse presentation again and complete workshop evaluations.
	9:30 a.m.	Make final presentation to the organization.
	10:00 a.m.	Hand off documents to workshop sponsor, process owner, and kaizen promotion office.
	10:30 a.m.	Workshop ends.

Figure 7.7 Typical kaizen workshop agenda.

include standard task, standard sequence, standard time, and standard work in process. The deviations we measure are likewise stated in these terms:

- Was each task performed as specified?
- Were the tasks performed in the specified sequence?
- Were the tasks performed in the specified cycle time?
- Were the tasks supported by the specified types and amounts of work-in-process inventory?

The answers to these questions provide Lean thinkers with data for analysis and improvement using the scientific method, or PDCA.

7.3.3 Check and Act: Develop Leader Standard Work

The reporting or "checking" method of hoshin involves a practice known as *leader standard work.*

Definition

Leader standard work is a system of regular visits to the gemba made by leaders and managers to check on both adherence to standard work and prog ress with improvement projects chartered by A3-Ts. A typical setup for the cycles of leader standard work is shown in Figure 7.8.

New Tool

Leader standard work is supported by *visibility walls. Visibility walls are collections of documents generated through the process of hoshin kanri, including value stream maps, A3-Ts, and statistics for the improvement activities chartered by the A3-Ts.* Walls are constructed for the value stream as a whole, for each loop in the value stream implementation plan, and for each process in the loop. They are the focal point of frequent review meetings focused only on those targets listed on the A3-T documents. Standing in front of a visibility wall, leaders and managers can see "at a glance" the status of a process and related improvement projects.

Example

In Figure 7.9 we see an example of a visibility wall constructed for a single implementation loop. In Figure 7.10 we see an example of a visibility wall constructed for a process. At tier 1, organizational leaders meet once a week for 1 to 2 hours to review the status of major improvement initiatives defined by their organization's A3-Ts.

Take Five

Take 5 minutes to think about these questions and to write down your answers:

1. What are value stream "loops," and why is it helpful to define them?
2. What techniques can be used to execute the plan, do, and check/act phases of strategy management, or *hoshin kanri?*

Leadership level	Work standard		Frequency
Corporate CEO	President's diagnosis	→	Annually
Divisional president	Leader standard work	→	Monthly
Value stream manager	Leader standard work	→	Weekly
Process manager	Leader standard work	→	Daily
Supervisor	Leader standard work	→	Hour by hour
Operator	Standard work	→	Minute by minute

Figure 7.8 Cycles of leader standard work.

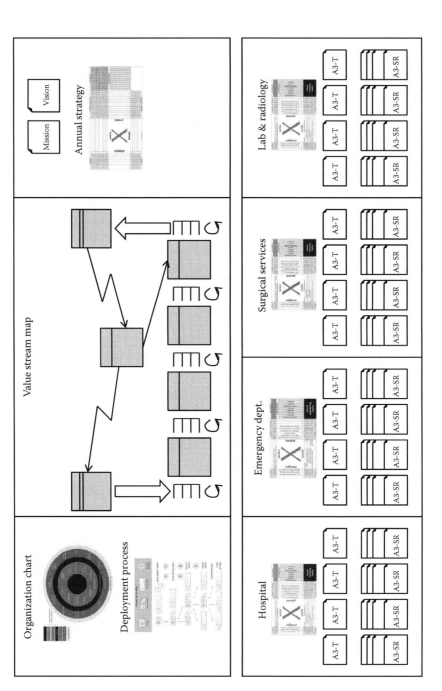

Figure 7.9 Value stream-level visibility wall: Process 4.

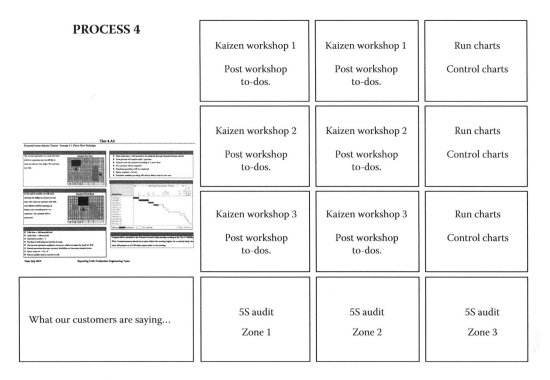

PROCESS 4

Figure 7.10 Process-level visibility wall.

7.4 WHERE TO BEGIN?

Healthcare is essentially a craft-based industry. When implementing the Lean value streams envisioned in Chapters 5 and 6, healthcare must often start from zero in terms of its current level of standardization. It is often said that before we create a Lean value stream, we must first stabilize processes. Lean processes must be highly responsive to multiple in-process controls that are triggered when processes cannot meet their takt times and whenever defects of any kind occur.

As we saw in Chapter 5, to achieve flow we must have the discipline to process patients one at a time in a first-in/first-out manner; no queue jumping is permitted when a process truly *flows*. In Chapter 6 we saw that in a Lean process where moving to the head of the line is permitted, queue jumping is nevertheless highly regulated with carefully sized buffers. Flow and pull are easier said than done; when processes are unstable, so many delays, defects, and other forms of waste occur that people spend a great deal of time putting out fires. Under such circumstances, FIFO lanes and buffers are impossible to maintain and heijunka, the leveling of production, is unthinkable.

Consequently, we can start just about anywhere, as long as we keep the long-term goal of achieving the future state: a series of *connected* patient flows. Many healthcare organizations naturally break down their implementation of future-state designs by concentrating on individual departments simultaneously. For example, it is common for the emergency department and the hospital to map their value streams independently; later, they may work together to integrate them into a single value stream. (Ambulance services are frequently contracted, so the initial loop in the value stream would probably be tackled last, after the organization itself has mastered Lean thinking and methods.)

This decentralized approach to mapping and building value streams can be very powerful and effective. Nevertheless, one should not lose sight of the ultimate goal, which is to provide care to patients in a continuous flow or, where that flow must be interrupted (for instance, as a result of different takt times in the emergency room and hospital), by means of pull systems.

7.5 SUMMARY

Future-state value stream maps are deceptively simple. To implement the future state, however, it is wise to break the value stream down into implementation "loops" or projects that can be managed separately, either in concert or in a series of projects. Frequently, value stream loops will correspond to traditional service lines under separate management, such as emergency services or inpatient services; however, in the future state they will be integrated into a more comprehensive flow. Loops may also correspond to the flows of ancillary and support services such as imaging and food services.

For each loop in your value stream, you should draft a project charter called an A3-T, which summarizes on one generous page the following key items:

- A quantitative description of the problem or opportunity for improvement
- Quantitative targets for lead-time reduction and quality improvement
- A cogent analysis of the causal mechanisms underlying the problem
- An outline of the proposed solution
- A project time line together with responsibilities for improvement activities
- A method for checking or monitoring progress and publishing results to your organization

Each A3-T comprises a complete Deming cycle of PDCA.

7.6 REFLECTIONS

Now that you have completed this chapter, take 5 minutes to think about these questions and write down your answers:

- What did you learn from reading this chapter that stands out as being particularly useful or interesting to you in healthcare?
- How do you feel about the idea of "loops" in the value stream?

- Do you have any questions about the topics presented in this chapter? If so, what are they?
- Are there any special obstacles in your mind or the minds of your colleagues to using the A3-T document system to document the Deming cycle of PDCA in healthcare?
- What information do you still need to understand fully the ideas presented?
- How can you get this information?
- Whom do you need to involve in this process?

Chapter 8

Reflections and Conclusions

8.1 REFLECTING ON WHAT YOU HAVE LEARNED

Key Point

An important part of learning is reflecting on what you have learned. Without this step, learning cannot take place effectively because few connections can be made to your existing knowledge and thus little useful information can be fixed in long-term memory. Now that you have come to the end of this book, we would like to ask you to reflect on what you have learned. We suggest you take 10 minutes to write down some quick answers to the following questions:

- Have you gotten what you wanted to get out of this book?
- Why or why not?
- What ideas, tools, and techniques have you learned that will be most useful in healthcare? How will they be useful?
- What ideas, tools, and techniques have you learned that will be least useful in your own life, at work, or at home? Why are they not useful?

8.2 APPLYING WHAT YOU HAVE LEARNED

8.2.1 Possibilities for Applying What You Have Learned

OVER VIEW

The way you decide to apply what you have learned will, of course, depend on your situation. If your organization is launching a full-scale Lean (or Six Sigma or Lean–Sigma) transformation program in which value stream mapping will be applied throughout the organization, you should have ample opportunity to apply what you have learned in this book in your own workplace. In this case, you may be included on a team of people who are responsible for mapping particular healthcare processes. You may have implementation time structured into your workday and may be responsible for reporting the results of your activities on a regular basis.

Key Point

At the other end of the spectrum, your organization may have no immediate plans to value stream map its clinical processes. In this case, the extent to which you can apply the method of value stream mapping will depend on how much control you have over your own schedule, work flow, and work area.

8.2.2 Applying Value Stream Mapping in Your Organization

Because value stream mapping appears to be simple on the surface, some managers mistakenly assume that application is also simple. As we have already mentioned, successful application requires top management participation. In addition, you need the right organization. Figure 8.1 describes a kaizen leadership team consisting of the CEO and direct reports, who set overall transformation strategy and monitor progress. The kaizen promotion office (KPO) is the "command center" for implementation activity and is led by the KPO vice president, who reports directly to the CEO of the organization. The KPO vice president is supported by a KPO director, who is directly responsible for Lean specialists, who are trained and certified in the methods of value stream mapping as well as many other Lean methods. Lean specialists are assigned to the organization's service lines and supporting administrative departments. In addition to Lean specialists, the KPO director is indirectly responsible for trained and certified kaizen directors who report directly to their service line and department leaders.

In addition to the right organization, you will need a detailed implementation plan. Figure 8.2 shows how you might plan an implementation focused on Lean healthcare, at the very core of which is standard work. This plan follows the plan–do–check–act (PDCA) logic we explored in Chapter 7 (see Figure 7.3 in that chapter). In the *plan* phase of implementation, the senior management is trained thoroughly in Lean techniques and organizes a kaizen promotion office. In the *do* phase of implementation, the KPO deploys standard work throughout the organization's key service lines. In the *check* phase, the KPO focuses on adherence to standard work by implementing 5S and

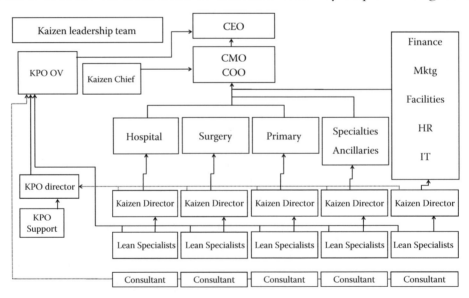

Figure 8.1 Kaizen leadership team. (From J. Michael Rona and Associates, LLC, doing business as Rona Consulting Group, copyright 2008–2013. http://www.rona consulting.com All rights reserved. Reprinted with permission.)

	Plan	Do	Check	Act
Kaizen Leadership Team	Find your sensei. Train and certify the Kaizen Leadership Team in standardization, standard work, and Lean thinking	Set up and staff the Kaizen Promotion Office system; Build and deploy a company wide improvement policy	Conduct weekly and monthly progress reviews of value stream process improvement metrics & financial results	Go "beyond budgeting" and focus on the process, not results; Conduct the first annual president's diagnosis using the Transformation Ruler
Kaizen Promotion Office	Train and certify a core group senior executives, Lean Specialists, and Kaizen Directors in standardization, standard work, and other Lean methods	• Value stream maps • Standard work • Quick setup • Five S; • Visual control • PDCA • Stop the line • Continuous flow	The number of modules expands to incorporate methods aimed at creating pull scheduling and supporting continuous improvement. By the end of this period the client is able to train and certify own experts in all relevant lean tools	• Kanban • Mistake-proofing • Systematic PDCA • Total productive maintenance; • Hoshin kanri • Value stream accounting • Transformation ruler
Service Line Leadership		Conduct time studies and value stream map the operating room, emergency room, inpatient flow, clinics, and ancillary services; Build standard work sheets, standard work combination sheets, percent load charts; Reduce setup times; redesign work flow; implement standard work and promote adherence w/five S	• Promote adherence through visual management • Implement patient safety and on system • Introduce PDCA problem solving documentation • Implement pull scheduling to link ancillary services and doctor referrals with healthcare operations:	Reduce setup times Redesign work flow Implement standard work and promote adherence w/five S; Improve continuously by implementing; • System PDCA throughout the organization • Mistake-proofing • Six sigma
Administrative and Support Leadership			Value stream map administrative operations, including accounting and human resources; Conduct time studies and build percent load charts; introduce Lean accounting practices	Improve continuously: • Systematic PDCA • Mistake-proofing
New Services and Facilities			Value stream map new service development process and establish a gated development system w/strict design review	Improve program management: • A3P and the QC matrix • Target costing • Kaizen costing; Improve continuously: • Systematic PDCA • Mistake-proofing
Value Chain Transformation			Measure quality, cost, & delivery; give feedback to suppliers	Reduce number of suppliers based upon performance criteria; Work with suppliers to eliminate waste, standardize work, and solve problems; Involve key suppliers upstream in the development of new services and facilities

Figure 8.2 Transformation road map.

visual management. In the *act* phase, the KPO focuses on introducing continuous improvement by training everyone in standardized problem-solving methods. The whole purpose of the plan is to deploy standard work, ensure adherence, and promote continuous improvement in all healthcare operations, in all supporting areas (including finance and human resource management), and, ultimately, in the organization's key suppliers.

8.2.3 Your Personal Action Plan

Key Point

You may or may not be in a management position that permits you to plan or implement standardization or standard work on a grand scale. Whatever your situation, *we suggest you create a personal action plan for how you will begin applying the information you have learned from this book.* You might start by referring to your own notes about the tools and techniques you think will be most useful to you and then writing down answers to the following questions:

■ What can I implement right now at work that will make my job easier, better, or more efficient?
■ What can I implement at home right now that will make activities there flow more easily or more efficiently?
■ How can I involve others at work and at home in the implementation of what I have learned?

When you have answered these questions, we suggest that you commit to completing the things you have written down in a specific period of time and to making a new plan at the end of that time period.

Key Point

In implementing anything, it is often good to start with something small that you can comfortably finish in the time you have allowed yourself. If the project is too ambitious or time consuming, you can easily get discouraged and give up.

Key Point

Also, projects you can work on for short periods of time whenever you get a chance are ideal in the beginning. For example, you might decide to value stream map a patient visit to the clinic or to the emergency department or operating room. Or you might implement standard work in the registration process and improve both lead time and the quality of information gathered from patients.

8.3 OPPORTUNITIES FOR FURTHER LEARNING

Here are some ways to learn more about standards and standardized work:

■ Find other books on this subject. Several of these are listed in the Appendix.
■ If your organization is already applying value stream mapping, visit other departments to see how they are using the tools and techniques.

- Find out how other healthcare organizations have applied value stream mapping to clinical value streams.
- Consider visiting local manufacturing companies with successful value stream mapping applications.

8.4 CONCLUSIONS

The approach of value stream mapping is a simple but powerful method for improvement in the healthcare environment. We hope this book has given you a taste of how this method can be helpful and effective for you in your work. Productivity Press and the Rona Consulting Group welcome your stories about how you apply value stream mapping in your own workplace.

Appendix

FURTHER READING ABOUT VALUE STREAM MAPPING

The following resources, available from Productivity Press, will provide you with additional education about various aspects of value stream mapping.

Beau Keyte and Drew Locher, *The Complete Lean Enterprise: Value Stream Mapping for Administrative and Office Processes* (New York: Productivity Press, 2004).

Mike Rother and John Shook, *Learning to See* (Brookline, MA: Lean Enterprise Institute, 1998).

Marc Taylor and Ian Baker, *Making Hospitals Work: How to Improve Patient Care While Saving Everyone's Time and Hospitals' Resources* (Herefordshire, UK: Lean Enterprise Academy, 2009).

FURTHER READING ABOUT LEAN HEALTHCARE

Thomas L. Jackson, editor, Lean Tools for Healthcare series, Rona Consulting Group and Productivity Press.

- *5S for Healthcare,* 2009. This guide imparts all the information needed to understand and implement this essential lean methodology for organization in the healthcare workplace. Includes helpful how-to-steps and practical examples taken directly from the healthcare industry.
- *Kaizen Workshops for Lean Healthcare,* 2012. This user-friendly volume describes what a "kaizen" improvement event entails and details all the phases necessary to conduct a successful kaizen workshop in healthcare. Covers planning, key roles, implementation, presentation of results, and ongoing follow-up.
- *Standard Work for Lean Healthcare,* 2011. This book explains how standard work can be used in healthcare to increase patient safety and reduce costs. It illustrates how standardization can help establish best practices for performing daily work and why it should be the cornerstone for all continuous improvement efforts. Presented in an easy-to-assimilate format, the book describes work in terms of cycle time, work in process, takt time, and layout.

Jeffrey C. Bauer, PhD, and Mark Hagland, *Paradox and Imperatives in Health Care: How Efficiency, Effectiveness, and E-Transformation Can Conquer Waste and Optimize Quality* (New York: Productivity Press, 2008). Bauer and Hagland explain why providers must draw upon internal resources to increase net revenue and provide the quality of care that payers and consumers demand. Through numerous case studies, the authors show how pioneering healthcare organizations are using performance improvement tools—including Lean management, Six Sigma, and the Toyota Production System—to produce excellent services as inexpensively as possible.

Mark Graban, *Lean Hospitals: Improving Quality, Patient Safety, and Employee Satisfaction,* second edition (New York: Productivity Press, 2011). This book explains why and how Lean can be used to improve quality, safety, and morale in a healthcare setting. Graban highlights the benefits of Lean methods and explains how Lean manufacturing staples such as value stream mapping can help hospital personnel identify and eliminate waste, effectively preventing delays for patients, reducing wasted motion for caregivers, and improving quality of care.

Naida Grunden, *The Pittsburgh Way to Efficient Healthcare: Improving Patient Care Using Toyota Based Methods* (New York: Productivity Press, 2008). Author Naida Grunden provides a hopeful look at how principles borrowed from industry can be applied to make healthcare safer and, in doing so, make it more efficient and less costly. The book presents a compilation of case studies from units in different hospitals around the Pittsburgh region that have applied industrial principles successfully, making patients safer and employees more satisfied.

USEFUL WEBSITES

Lean Blog. A blog founded by author Mark Graban about Lean in factories, hospitals, and the world around us. http://www.leanblog.org/

John Grout's Mistake Proofing Center. Shingo Prize-winner John Grout's collection of three websites devoted to poka yoke (mistake proofing), a key technique for 5S and Lean operations generally. An entire website within the center is devoted to healthcare applications of mistake proofing.

www.ronaconsulting.com. The official website of series editor Thomas L. Jackson and his partners at the Rona Consulting Group. (http://www.ronaconsulting.com)

www.productivitypress.com. The website of Productivity Press, where you may order the books mentioned here, among many others about Lean manufacturing, total quality management, and total productive maintenance. (www.productivitypress.com)

Index